THE DOGMA OF RUFUS

THE DOGMA OF RUFUS

A CANINE GUIDE TO EATING, SLEEPING, DIGGING, SLOBBERING, SCRATCHING, AND SURVIVING WITH HUMANS

Written by

Rufus, an Old Dog

with the help of Larry, Zack, and Joey Arnstein

Skyhorse Publishing

Skyhorse Publishing books may be purchased in bulk at special discounts
for sales promotion, corporate gifts, fund-raising, or educational
purposes. Special editions can also be created to specifications.
For details, contact the Special Sales Department, Skyhorse Publishing,
307 West 36th Street, 11th Floor, New York, NY 10018 or
info@skyhorsepublishing.com.

Skyhorse® and Skyhorse Publishing® are registered trademarks of
Skyhorse Publishing, Inc.®, a Delaware corporation.

Visit our website at www.skyhorsepublishing.com

10 9 8 7 6 5 4 3 2 1

Library of Congress Cataloging-in-Publication Data is available on file.

ISBN: 978-1-62087-604-6

Printed in China

For Walter Frederick Morrison, inventor of the Frisbee

CONTENTS

Section 2: Troubleshooting

INTRODUCTION

Hello, my name is Rufus. I am a dog. I ask you young dogs to temporarily put on hold all tail and squirrel chasing, leg humping, and other important daily activities, while I share with you the wisdom I've gained over a long life.

Why should you read this book? No one can guarantee success, but in these pages lies a collection of ancient wisdom passed down through the years from dog to dog. Correctly mastering the techniques outlined in the following chapters can help you maximize your potential to obtain food, mark your territory with greater efficacy, fetch and return tennis balls with greater professionalism than you've ever imagined, secure the blessings of the best sleeping locations, and lead a more meaningful dog life.

You will also gain intimate knowledge of the human condition, and be better prepared to help them lead a less pathetic existence.

I know we've just gone over this, but for those of you whose focus has already been compromised, I ask you again to please stop leg humping for the duration of this book, or at least until the next chapter break.

Rufus

HUMAN-DOG DICTIONARY

alphabetize (*v.*) 1. unnecessary form of human organization. 2. something we're not going to do here. Instead, check out your house to see if anyone has dropped any food, or if you can guilt-trip anyone into to giving you a treat.

garden (*n.*) 1. great place to dig up. 2. great place to bury bones. 3. great all-around place to dig up flowers, play, bury stuff, roll around in. 4. can't say enough about this place. (*v.*) 1. to prepare hard dirt into soft area for dogs, to put flower seeds into, weed, enhance soil with special enriched earth so it's even better to dig up.

newspaper (*n.*) soft, very eatable, chewable thing suitable for gnawing, chomping, and spreading around the house.

greet (*v.*) 1. to jump up on. 2. to lick the face of. 3. to knock over.

happy (*adj.*) 1. natural state of all dogs. 2. state only dogs can show humans how to achieve. 3. what dogs feel when it's time to eat, sleep, play, or go for a walk. 4. did I mention eating? 5. do you happen to have anything I can eat right now?

couch (*n.*) 1. great place to stretch out and sleep on, especially after an hour of romping in the mud or digging in the garden (see above).

bone (*n.*) a thing that would have been good when the meat was on it, but the humans have eaten all the meat. You end up chomping on it frantically, trying to get the meat which isn't there anymore, while they congratulate themselves on what a great thing they've done for you.

begging (*n.*) human word that does not at all describe what we do, which is merely *looking* at human food nobody seems to be interested in. *Observing* the food; concentrating on it; focusing on it; possibly looking up at the humans, then back at the food. Maybe whimpering a little, but *not* begging.

SECTION ONE:
THE FUNDAMENTALS

Chapter 1
HUMAN FOOD: OUR CENTRAL PURPOSE (A MISSION STATEMENT)

There are two kinds of food: human food and dog food. Human food is better. That's why they call their food, "food," and ours, "dog food."

"I wouldn't feed that to my dog!" What does that tell you?

There are three ways of getting human food:

1) Jump up on the table when nobody's looking and just go for it. This is known as the "grab-and-go." (see Fig. 1.1) It is very effective but is always followed by a lot of angry human shouting.

2) Wait for something to fall from the table, then scarf it down immediately. If it falls to the floor, it's yours.

3) Keenly observe the food. This can work, but for some reason humans don't like it. On the other hand, dogs have perfected observing food for thousands of years, it's in your

Fig. 1.1: The Grab-and-Go

DNA, so just do it. You know how. Use your ears, your eyes, and if necessary, whimper.

> **HISTORICAL SIDEBAR** – Some say this strange practice of throwing away food that has touched the floor dates back thousands of years and is based on human mythology and dark magic superstitions. Whatever the origin, it is simply one of many stupid things humans do that we should never try to understand.

Most of what we do will be based around our central purpose of obtaining the human food, or at the very least, larger quantities of dog food. While at times we may thoroughly enjoy the food the humans label as dog food, especially those biscuit treat things, we needn't let our humans know this. We must, at all times, appear to be experiencing great suffering.

List of Good Reasons Not to Eat Human Food

.   .   .

Learning about Human Food

Categories: Deliciousness Ranking, Difficulty of Obtainment, etc.

Chips and Crackers: This category involves a wide range of mysterious, bite-sized snacks. They are mysterious because we dogs normally don't get to really know what they are because we tend to receive them via throw, and thus have swallowed them entirely before ever getting to fully examine their contents. Nonetheless, they are usually quite delicious, and most important, very high on the likelihood of obtainment. This is because a human feels that he has so many of them, due to their bite-sizedness, that he can afford to share just one or two with the dog.

Pizza: You will likely not experience such generosity from the humans when it comes to larger foods such as pizza. In contrast with many other human foods that are created during at least an hour of preparation in the kitchen, pizza appears suddenly at the door, immediately filling the room up with an overwhelming sweet odor. While it is rare that the humans will share this food, it sometimes will linger in a box accessibly close to the edge of a table, and thus can be achieved through "grab-and-go" (see Fig. 1.1.).

Everything else: Since it's all so good, there isn't much point in analyzing the categories any further, not to mention it's getting me all worked up and I'm not sure I will be able to continue working if I don't stop talking about human food immediately. Just do your best to eat as much as possible and don't worry too much about what it is you may be eating. Surely, it will be an amazing experience.

Dining Etiquette: Why Is a French Word Necessary?

Any activity which requires a French word to describe it is probably something dogs don't want to be involved in. Of course I'm not talking about eating, I'm talking about "dining." Right away you know there's something wrong. Wherever "dining" is happening, there are "table manners," which isn't French, it's British. Britain is also a suspect nation, except for the fact that they seem to like dogs there. Even the Queen of England likes dogs, but if you have a place like Buckingham Palace with a lot of "grounds" as your home, you have to have dogs running around there, don't you? And you need somebody you can talk to besides other members of the Royal Family.

Unfortunately, the concept of dining etiquette and table manners is not confined to these faraway places where you can't understand what they're saying, and I include France in that statement. It can happen right here, if there are "guests" present. When this happens, suddenly the "good" silverware comes out of the drawer where it has not caused any trouble for months. "Good" means you can't cut anything with the knives, the forks are awkward, and the spoons are too small. Also, all of a sudden the food has long and confusing names.

Meatloaf is transformed into Beef Wellington, and in place of frozen peas, corn, and carrots, you have individual vegetables with their own names. "Do ya want any more?" becomes, "Would you care for some more *Duck a la Orange?*" I have heard, too many times, the reply, "Oh, no thank you—it's so delicious, but I'm watching my weight." Well, I'm also watching your weight, and guess what? There's too much of it. Here's what I'd like to hear instead: "Oh, no thank you, but my dog will have some." I bet that's what the Queen of England says, and the Duchess of Kent then directs the waitpersons to give a generous helping to the Queen's corgis.

One Bowl, Many Mouths

As you already know, the number of dogs who can comfortably eat out of one bowl at the same time is limited only by the size of the bowl and the size of the dogs. If there's only a small amount of food, then the first dog who gets to the bowl will scarf down most of it, so you always want to be first dog if possible. This means being aware and alert to the sound of food being emptied into a bowl at all times.

By contrast, humans aren't comfortable sticking their heads together into the same bowl or plate at the same time. It's partly on account of their short and inadequate tongues, but also because they aren't comfortable with anything remotely natural.

Instead they have individual plates; one for each human who is theoretically sharing their mealtime in convivial eating and drinking. If that isn't sufficiently bizarre, they won't use those famous opposable thumbs of theirs to pick up the food and shovel it into their mouths efficiently. Oh, no. They have silverware, specifically knives, forks, and spoons, sometimes more than one of each: a "salad fork," for example (although why any sentient being other than a rabbit or a snail would want to eat a salad is unknown). The result of all these needless individual plates, bowls, cups, glasses, and silverware is that there's a need to "clean up" when the meal, pointlessly elongated by talking and drinking, is over.

Part of the reason for human suffering, and why humans at this stage in their evolution can't reach the higher levels of blissfulness that we dogs know, comes from this incessant need to mix things that really should be separate. In this example, we are talking about mixing eating with talking. The humans think that mixing different activities together will somehow double their enjoyment of these activities, when in fact, while trying to concentrate on eating and conversing simultaneously, they end up not really appreciating either. This problem is not restricted to the "dining" table. Take walking. Your typical human does not find the act of simply walking outside to be entertaining enough, so they stick earphones in their ears and listen to music while they walk. Thus, while we dogs are fully enjoying the simple pleasure of walking, the humans are half walking, half listening, and probably sending a text message at the same time. And they wonder why they spend most of their lives in therapy!

Getting back to the more important subject of the end of the human meal: of course we can help with the cleanup, and in fact do the whole thing ourselves by licking their plates

Dog enjoying a walk

Confused human multitasking

clean. Since they won't do this themselves, there are usually excellent bits of food and gravy left for us.

When we're done cleaning up, there's no good reason why the plates, which are now very clean, cannot be stacked in cabinets, ready for the next meal, but unsurprisingly, the humans insist on doing their own "official" post-dog cleaning, usually by putting everything in a "dishwasher," with which they then waste large quantities of water, noxious chemical soap, and energy, all of which they're running out of on the Great Dog's Earth, at an astounding pace. They do the same thing with their clothes, which they insist on throwing into similar machines just when they're beginning to smell interesting.

Humans' lives are so full of this kind of useless activity, it's no wonder they need to relax by altering their consciousness with alcohol.

Chapter 2
"OUR FOOD": ALSO GOOD, BUT DON'T GET DISTRACTED!

Eating and chewing are often thought of as part of the same process, and sometimes they are, but not always. For example, if you can basically inhale your food in one swallow, you should do that. If you don't, there's no guarantee the food will still be there a minute from now. Another dog could suddenly appear and snatch it from you, or a human could suddenly decide to take it away. Lots of bad things could happen if you hesitate.

Who chews their food? Humans, that's who, because they don't appreciate their food. Evidence shows a human will often not eat all the food on the table, or even on their own plate! While the food is in front of the human, waiting to be eaten, he will often talk with other humans, pushing the food around on the plate, cutting it into unnecessarily small pieces, and even then, chewing before swallowing. If you can swallow a piece of food, there's no reason to chew it—lots of reasons not to.

On the other hand, sometimes you have a bone with meat on it, so it must be chewed before it can be swallowed. Then you need to break out your chewing skills. You'll probably need to remove the bone from your dish and put it on the floor so you can put a paw on it for stability. If the bone isn't too big, sometimes you can crack it with a powerful jaw crunch, which can be very satisfying.

Young dog experiencing important chewing event

Humans don't get this. They will leave a bone with quite a lot of meat on it, because they're not willing to pick it up and go *after* it. You see this a lot when they're having guests over, or if it's a date or something where they don't want to make a lot of bone-crunching noises and have meat juices running down their chin—which is really part of the enjoyment of eating, possibly the best, or at least second best after swallowing. But you know? That's perfectly okay. We are right there, ready to take over finishing that bone.

We communicate our readiness by sitting at a polite distance (not too far!) from the table, and staring at the food. Concentrate on that food with *intensity*. Focus, focus, focus!

Our message to humans: Keep yourselves dainty and pretty! Don't let

Dog focusing with great intensity on food (not shown)

any of those meat juices trickle down your chin and stain your dress. Let *us* handle the difficult part.

Conclusion: As you can see, I have gotten off subject again, and have begun discussing human food, although this chapter is about "Dog" food. This is an advanced teaching technique that I have employed to help you understand the importance of not forgetting about our Central Purpose! (See Chapter 1.)

Chapter 3
SLEEPING: EASY TO PICK UP, A LIFETIME TO MASTER

In the sleep field of study, we once again find that humans have made a mess of the terminology, causing unnecessary confusion for many young puppies. They have invented the phrase "dog bed." While there is nothing wrong with enjoying a slumber in what the humans refer to as the "dog bed," the phrase really means nothing. There are so many places where we can and must sleep: couches, human beds, grassy patches of shade, even a pile of shoes is just as much a "dog bed" as anything else.

Please refer to the following instructional diagrams illustrating basic and advanced sleeping techniques:

Fig. 3.1: Dog sleeping (basic)

Fig. 3.2 Dog sleeping (advanced)

You should have no trouble with the basic position, and as far as the advanced position goes, there's just no substitute for practice. You must make time in your daily schedule for sleep practice.

Here again we may find some insight into the plight of the human. At this point in their evolution, humans tend to believe that sleeping must occur at specified sleeping times, in specified sleeping places, and for specified time periods, based on what appear to be completely random calculations. The humans seem to think that sleeping more than the absolute minimum necessary for basic organ function is a bad thing. The humans even set mechanical buzzing sounds, programmed to interrupt their sleep at its best, most excellent moment, in some sort of ritual of self-castigation. At the point that this buzzing sound occurs, which can at times affect our dog sleep as well unfortunately, the humans leave their designated sleeping space and may not engage in sleeping for hours, or even the rest of the day!

Which Bed, Exactly, Is "Our Bed"?

Some humans, especially when they've invested in the dreaded "dog bed," can be very insistent on when and where you should sleep. Disregard. If you must, go to sleep in the dog bed, then wait until the humans are asleep. Then join them in their bed. In the morning you all wake up, together, in their/your bed. (See Fig. 3.3).

They will eventually accept this.

Fig. 3.3: Dog sleeping where a dog should sleep

A List of Places Not Appropriate for Us to Sleep

.   .   .

NAPS

There are three kinds of naps: the catnap, the dog nap, and the human nap.

Let's dispense with the catnap right away. As you can see, it has the word "cat" embedded in it, so definitionally it's already bad. Also, you think the cat is asleep, so you're tempted to relax, but you can never be absolutely sure if a cat is really asleep, or for that matter, really dead (a subject discussed at length in Cats: An Evolutionary Mistake).

Next we come to the dog nap, a good and necessary thing. You need to conserve your energy for important activities like eating and welcoming visitors, which require lots of energy. So you have to stock up on sleep during the day.

Then there's the human nap, which is more of a nuanced thing. If a human needs to nap a little to renew his energy before taking you to the park and maybe throwing a Frisbee around with you, that's good. On the other

Fig. 3.4: Dog catching a few in the afternoon

hand, the human could be taking you to the park *right now*, *instead of* napping. The dilemma is: permit the human to nap, or wake him up immediately? Tough call.

Finally, let me conclude by presenting an instructional visual aid that may help you better understand the concept of "Dog Resting." When we are not sleeping, eating, or running around having fun, it is essential to do a good amount of resting. Please see Figure 3.5 and commence resting practice now.

Fig. 3.5: These dogs are not napping, just resting

Chapter 4
MARKING YOUR TERRITORY: THIS TREE IS MINE. ALSO, THIS FENCE.

Humans make this process much more complicated than it needs to be, building fences and creating armies to conquer land that other humans have marked, when all one needs to do is simply pee. Consider the following instructional diagrams:

Fig. 4.1: Marking territory, complicated

Fig. 4.2: Marking territory, simple

Despite its simplicity, marking your territory is extremely important. You can't just pee and forget. Another dog will pee over your pee. You cannot allow this. You have to smell everywhere and always have enough in your bladder to pee over another dog's pee. While you can never allow another dog to pee where you have peed, it's perfectly alright to pee over another dog's marker, especially if it's within your territory, and even if it isn't.

A small note—the territory that you want to mark is your extended territory, or really, not your territory. The territory that truly is your territory—like your house, your bed, etc. —that territory you don't have to, and shouldn't, mark. The humans

Fig. 4.3: Dog marking territory (basic)

**Fig. 4.4: Dog marking territory (advanced).
Note advanced tail position, aesthetically
counterbalanced to pee stream**

will not appreciate it if you do. That territory is officially
yours, nothing else needed.

Once again: your bed is your bed, your human's bed is
also your bed; no one is going to dispute that. You *do not* have
to mark it.

My Daily Schedule

Of course doing the same thing every day at the same time
is pretty dull, and I don't recommend it. That said, puppies
may want to know what they can look forward to schedule-
wise as adult dogs. So this is pretty much what mine is like:

5:30 AM: Wake-up time for the humans! Lick their faces, push your cold nose into their ears, and take other necessary measures to get them up and out of bed. Doesn't matter if their alarm clock didn't buzz yet.

5:35 AM: Human opens back door for emergency use.

5: 45 AM: Pre-breakfast Pee, Poop, and Territory-marking Walk. Your markers will need refreshing from yesterday. If you see any place you didn't hit then, hit it now.

6:30 AM: Dog Breakfast.

6:35 AM: Wow, that was fast. Of course, they didn't feed me much, they never do.

6:35–7:00 AM: Agonizing wait while they do stuff in their bathroom. What do they *do* in there?

7:00 AM: Finally: Human Breakfast. Monitor closely. Scraps may fall to the floor. Also, they won't have time to clean their plates and bowls, so be ready to clean that up for them.

7:15–8:30 AM: Morning nap. Don't allow yourself to fall into too deep a sleep, because of Snack Opportunities you could miss out on. Anytime your humans are awake is a potential Snack Opportunity.

8:30–8:40 AM: Morning nap break. Check around to see if there's any food you might have missed while napping, reposition for remainder of morning nap.

8:40–10:00 AM: Morning nap, part two.

10:00–10:30 AM: Mid-morning Snack Opportunity. Be sure to show your readiness for any kind of snack or treat.

10:30–Noon: Mid-morning walk. Time to refresh your markers, also be alert for Social Opportunities, butt-sniffing, etc.

Noon: Lunchtime!!

12:30–2:30 PM: Early afternoon nap, first half.

2:30–4:00 PM: After checking for scraps that may have fallen to the floor while humans tried to sneak in any secret eating activity while you slept, resume nap, possibly in a different place.

4:00 PM–5:30 PM: Park time!! If your human has forgotten this important part of the day, make sure you remind him. Stand by the door and stare back and forth between the door and your human.

6:00 PM: Dinner: The Big One! After you get your food, the humans will be cooking, or if they're lazy, ordering out. Monitor all this activity closely. By now the humans will have started drinking, so be alert and ready for any food falling from their table and any uneaten, extra food they might foolishly consider throwing away. If necessary, stand between them and the garbage and prevent access.

Note: *never* allow them to throw food away, but if you fail, there is a back-up: knock over the garbage can in the alley where it's eventually dumped, and see what's going on in there.

7:30 PM–8:00 PM: Evening walk: poop, refresh markers.

8:00 PM–10:00 PM: Position yourself on couch for some TV watching with the humans. Note: They will often go to the kitchen during commercial breaks—you know what this means: follow them.

10:00 PM: Winding down towards bedtime. While humans do whatever they do in the bathroom to prepare for this, start some preemptive barking to alert the neighborhood of any potential threats, and get the Dog Neighborhood Watch Alert System ready for nighttime activity.

10:30 PM: Position yourself in bed, begin snoring.

Chapter 5

CHASING BALLS, FRISBEES, ETC.: AN UNDENIABLY CAPTIVATING EXPERIENCE

Another reason why humans are such pathetic, unhappy beings is that they overcomplicate even the simplest of things, such as games. For a dog, a game is about the pleasure of playing. We see something get thrown and we run with all our hearts after that thing until we have that thing in our mouth, then we bite on that thing. That's it. Nothing else needed. The humans, on the other hand, complicate things by adding innings, and clocks, and yard-measuring chains, and technical fouls, and offsides. Offsides! It's no wonder they get stressed out even while playing! If there is a dog chasing a ball somewhere in the world right now, you can rest assured knowing that this lucky dog is not concerned with going offsides.

I promise you this dog is not concerned about being offsides.

As simple as our games are, it is important to analyze some technicalities of chasing on a deeper level.

For example, it is part of the Great Dog's Divine Plan that dogs chase bicycles. It's called "natural selection." The way this plays out on the plains of the Serengeti is that the lions chase down the slowest, weakest gazelles, and eat them. It is the same with bicyclists, who also travel in herds. It is good for the gazelles that their weakest members are culled by lions, and it is also good for bicyclists that we bring down the stragglers in the bicycle herds.

That said, you should also know, my puppies, that chasing down and bagging a cyclist is one of the truly great pleasures in a dog's life. Humans present no challenge. They are slow and not used to running from predators. And it's been thousands of years since they could climb a tree in a hurry. But a human on a bicycle can really fly. Chasing one down is much more like chasing a gazelle, or an antelope.

Regarding the Frisbee, there is a difficult moment when you bring it back to your human. We have been dealing with this perplexing paradox since the Great Dog created sticks. You want to chase it down again, but in order to do that, you have to give it up. Let me repeat this one more time: You must give it back in order to win possession of it again. And it's yours now, so you don't want to. Perhaps the following diagram will help clear up the confusion:

Fig. 5.1: Chase Frisbee, return Frisbee

Your human grabs it, which only makes you want to hang on more tightly, which turns into a game of tugging, which you also enjoy. But you must let go after a bit of a tussle if you want to chase it down again. Sometimes that's hard to remember, but it must be so.

With respect to chasing balls, let us consider golf.

In golf, humans are not always competing against each other. Instead, they compete against themselves, writing down how many shots they've taken and getting very angry. It really is a gift to them if you find one of their golf balls after they've hit it, and just run away with it. They may not like it at the time, but they will be grateful later. When they have no more golf balls, they will be forced to just enjoy walking around outdoors. Or riding around in those ridiculous "golf carts." Which you can also chase, but they're so slow, there's not much point. Instead, wait for a kid on a skateboard. Now *that* is worthwhile.

Chapter 6
LICKING: WHAT, WHERE, WHEN, AND WHY

While there are good arguments to be made for licking all things equally, there are others who argue that your most intense licking should be reserved for precious moments. For example, if a particularly squeamish human were to enter your domicile, this may be an opportune time to lay out a good surprise licking. The following might be an appropriate strategy: A human social event of some sort is occurring. Approach each of the guests politely and with restraint. Come close to each human and accept their physical greeting, but do not touch any of them. When you finally get to the squeamish one, the one with the fanciest clothes and most carefully arranged hairdo, that's when you really lay on a good, slimy lick, right to the face if possible and jump all over them to get your fur on their fancy jacket. This will help this human relax and enjoy life a little bit more, and will make you the star of the party.

In addition to social licking, there is also self-based licking. We do this for hygienic reasons, first aid, to fight boredom, and because we can. Most self-licking should come easy to you, but there are those hard-to-reach places that can drive a dog mad.

Fortunately, there are role models:

This mad genius, Rex Montgomery III, was gold medalist in Oral Gymnastics in the 1984 Dog Olympics in Barcelona.

This competitor, Wolfgang von Holstengeshlafen, took home the bronze medal for Switzerland, but was later famously disqualified for blood doping.

While we can't all be champions, it would be a shame not to put to use the incredible tongues we have. With the exception of frogs, we have the most awesome tongues in the animal kingdom. Even if you don't go pro, practice. Hone your skills.

Lick others, lick yourself, lick up, lick down, lick left, lick right, lick, lick, lick!

Q & A (First of Several)

Q: When is the best time to start barking?

A: There is no one, best time. Any time is a good time to bark, any reason is a good reason.

Q: But my humans don't like it . . .

A: What humans don't understand is that when it comes to barking, it's use it or lose it. If you didn't keep your barking muscles well-toned with occasional, random barking, they might not be there for you when you really need them, like when the house is under attack by terrorists masquerading as UPS guys. If you couldn't defend your house, the humans would be very sorry. *Boom!* No house, no humans.

Q: Is there a best time to stop barking?

A: Not really. However, after a minimum of a few minutes of steady barking, it may be necessary to conclude, once the threat has passed. You don't want to over-bark because you could bark yourself out, needlessly exposing your humans to risk.

Q: How long before I can relax?

A: Stay alert for not less than three hours following the initial threat, and respond without hesitation when any other dog in the Neighborhood Emergency Alert Network starts to bark.

Q: Are dog treats always a good thing?

A: This is a more complex situation than it appears at first sniff. One not-so-good thing about dog treats is that they're normally used as a bribe for certain behaviors, which may or may not be good. Sitting down, lying down, rolling over are all used to establish dominance over a dog, and while the treat itself may be good, the whole idea of command-and-obey is problematic.

Q: Is there anything else wrong with a dog treat?

A: If your human gives you too many treats, he can get the idea that you have been fed, and not feed you. This is wrong. A dog treat is not a meal, it's just a treat. You have not been fed. You deserve a regular, full meal, preferably their food, not "dog food." As a reminder, a dog treat, although it may be provided at the same time when the humans eat their food, is not an acceptable alternative to getting some real human food. The treat should be eaten as quickly as possible, without losing track of the main focus.

Q: What if I am not a dog, but rather a human? Can I still continue reading and enjoying this book?

A: While we appreciate your interest in this book, unfortunately, the answer is no, you cannot continue reading this book.

The information contained in this book is not only private material intended only for dog use, but wouldn't make sense to you anyway, as your brains have not evolved yet to the level necessary to understand.

Q: I am a human and I feel offended by this comment about my brain not being as evolved as a dog's brain.

A: Let me explain. Take this concept of you being "offended." This is yet another overly complicated emotion that only humans would experience. Dogs don't get "offended" and thus cannot suffer from being "offended." There are all sorts of these basically negative emotions that humans still have that dogs have overcome through evolution—embarrassment, greed, anxiety, envy, hate; we don't have any of these problems. Therefore, what I have said in this book regarding your brains is not intended to offend, but is rather an obvious, honest assessment of the current state of affairs.

Q: I am really enjoying this book. May I send dog treats to the author as a show of appreciation?

A: Yes. Preferred treats are chicken flavor, or any of those shaped like bones; multi-colored treats are not necessary.

Q: I am a cat, and I just want you to know I think this book sucks!

A: Your opinion is not welcome here.

Q: I am a hard-working, bike-riding, morning newspaper delivery boy, and I was wondering if there is anything I can do to get you and your readers to lay off a bit?

A: No more questions for today, thanks!

Chapter 7
BITING: ASK QUESTIONS LATER

Although it is difficult to understand why, we aren't supposed to bite everything and everyone we please. Though this is totally contradictory to the laws of nature as we see them, we must respect this condition of our situation if we are to obtain the most delicious of the human foods. The question of what and whom to bite can be confusing and complex, but with the right guidance, can be simple to understand. The key word is "self-interest." Sometimes what we want is not necessarily in our self-interest when evaluated from a non-biased, external point of view. For example, biting the person who is most likely to give us human food is not in our self-interest. Biting an anonymous mailman, preferably one who does not directly service our food providers, in the presence of no authority relevant to our food provision, on the other hand, may be very much in our self-interest.

What humans don't understand, is that biting is not really an expression of aggression or dislike or anger. Biting is just our way of saying "I want to bite you." But, just for the sake of getting along with the humans, you will need to restrain your biting instinct, at least around your local food providing humans. If you are a young dog, and you are having trouble with this, it may be helpful to practice here before heading out into the real world where there may be consequences for uncontrolled biting, the most humiliating and de-dogulating of which is the muzzle. Please stare at the following pictures and practice resisting the temptation to bite when not appropriate:

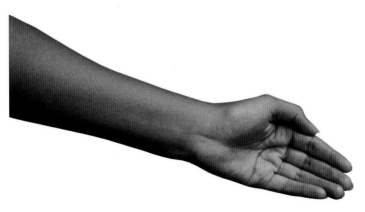

Don't do it.

Resist! Resist!

No! No! Oh-so-tempting, but you must refrain!

Okay. Go for it!

Chapter 8
SLOBBERING: FUNDAMENTALS TO ADVANCED TECHNIQUES

As we hinted at in the chapter on licking, many humans are very tense. We know that part of our jobs as dogs is to help the humans relax. If you happen to be a very slobbery breed of dog, you have a very clear window into seeing which of the humans at your everyday access is suffering most from tension. When you approach a certain human and find that he/she reacts with great intensity, making loud noises, possibly jumping up onto a chair to try to avoid contact with your mouth and slobber, you know that this particular human is greatly suffering from tension. This human has his understanding of the world so warped that he actually believes that your innocent slobber is something to be greatly feared.

As you can imagine, a person like this goes through life in constant fear of everything, unable to enjoy the simple pleasures that you and I take for granted. It is your duty to help this person. The best thing you can do is to help him conquer his fear of the outside world by letting some of your slobber connect with his leg perhaps, or her arm, or even with his shoe, or her purse. Do not let him slither away by climbing up the chair; you must connect! This won't have an immediate revolutionary effect on the person, but bit by bit, as he realizes that the things in this world he fears do not actually cause his death or illness, slowly, he will become a less fearful person. He will never reach the level of life satisfaction of a dog, but your contribution will be crucial. Your job is not over. Remember this person, and continue the treatment at all possible future opportunities.

This type of therapy is something you are uniquely able to administer, so you must take you responsibilities seriously. Fundamental slobbering techniques involve identifying the types of foods that most produce this helpful substance we call slobber. Advanced techniques include especially long slobber streams. This is not something you will be able to achieve right away, but after some dedicated practice, you will learn how to keep especially long slobber streams hanging from your mouth, and prevent them from falling to the floor. It is a delicate balancing act, but you must keep the slobber attached to the mouth until a human is available for deposit. In an emergency situation in which no leg or human personal item is available for slobber transfer, you may use books, and furniture as well.

Though you may have already found that this fun and required pastime comes quite naturally to you, there is always room for improvement. Making a clear, organized list of one's values is a powerful tool for life enrichment, and a dog should remember to make slobbering at your fullest, messiest potential a high priority. In striving to achieve an excellent technique, a puppy may be able to accomplish great things.

For example, sharing your slobber with your human's evening attire may ensure that they forgo their intended outing to stay home, feed you, and maybe scratch behind your ears. An expensive-looking dress would suggest intentions to leave you at home and go out. Make sure you are prepared to get some good slobber on such a dress should you see one laid out on the bed or being worn by your human.

Please observe the following slobbering dogs for inspiration:

Regulating Your Body Temperature

Because of the complex nature of dogs, we self-regulate our body temperature in various ways. If we become overheated, probably the best solution is to jump into a river, lake, swimming pool, or even just a little inflatable kiddie pool in the front yard. Your next step is to shake yourself dry. Do this next to a human being, so they can share in the cooling-off experience, even if they don't appear to want to.

If it's a hot day and you're outside, the sun will beat down on your fur and pretty soon you'll be overheated again. This is why you should go *inside* before shaking off. It will also help cool off the inside of the house, which is too hot.

Good technique, but this dog should be inside.

Actually, the very best place for cooling off on a hot day is a puddle of mud. If there's mud handy, definitely roll around in it till you're completely covered, *then* go inside and share it with your humans.

There's no better place to share your mud than a couch or, ideally, a freshly made bed. Already the sheets and pillow cases are cool, and when you add mud to that, the fresh coolness of the experience is truly unique. This is such a better way of cooling off than air conditioning, you'd think humans would have discovered it by now, but since they haven't, we need to educate them by bringing it inside and sharing.

The other method we have of cooling off is letting our tongues hang out of our mouths and panting. Humans don't have long tongues, so they have to sweat. This is the only time they smell good, but of course they feel they have to get the good smell off as soon as possible and replace it with the unpleasant smells of soap and shampoo products.

Anyway, panting with our tongues out generally leads to slobbering, a healthful, temperature-regulating technique.

Once again, since adult humans can no longer drool, it's up to us to share our slobber with them by licking their faces when we have more than we need, which frankly, is most of the time. They may try to discourage you from doing this, but as with most things which are enjoyable, humans have a very difficult time enjoying it.

They want your slobber, they're just too embarrassed to ask.

Now, go practice, but save a little of the slobber for the next chapter, Welcoming Guests.

Dog self-regulating body temperature

Chapter 9
WELCOMING GUESTS: TRY NOT TO HYPERVENTILATE

When humans come to visit each other it is customary that . . . *OH MY GOD! Someone's at the door! Somebody has come to see me! Or they're here for any other reason, it doesn't matter! This is unbelievably thrilling! I'm so excited I just may pee on the floor, or dislocate my hindquarters from wagging my tail!*

This amazing event absolutely requires me to jump up on to the human, or wait . . . WAIT! There are multiple humans, each one of whom must be jumped on and/or knocked down and slobbered on!

Uncontrollable excitement is a perfectly natural reaction to the astonishing event of a human, known or unknown, walking through a door into your house. Their arrival shouldn't come as a complete surprise in the sense that you should have heard or smelled or sensed the approach of the humans no less than one hundred yards from the door, but then again, you may have been sleeping, and some humans are sneaky and quiet. You can make up for your lack of vigilance by bounding across the floor when the door opens and leaping through the air at them. It's the least you can do.

Probably your human is saying meaningless stuff like, "No!" and "Down!" but as discussed in Sometimes but Rarely-Asked Questions, these words lack any real, operational meaning.

You must ignore these instructions and give the full welcome. Why? Because humans are so emotionally closed off that they cannot express their emotions for themselves, so you must take up the slack. Most likely, even if your humans are close family relatives who haven't seen each other in ages, they will probably greet each other with a firm handshake, a couple of comments about the weather, and some pointless questions about what the other one has been up to recently. They don't even want to know the answers to these questions, they just don't really know how to welcome someone. We do. For example, a human would never think to pick up a valuable, designer shoe in its mouth as an invitation to a friendly game of tug-of-war to liven the greeting experience. Today's homework assignment is to find an expensive designer shoe and put it in a secret place so it will be ready for a more exciting, joyful greeting process.

Get to it!

Chapter 10
CHASING CARS: "THE WHITE WHALE"

Call me Rufus. I am not here to judge another dog, or say what is right, or what is good. I come here not to say what is or what should be. But, I do know suffering. I do remember pain. I do come here to say: Let the car pass. Do not pursue. Do not give chase. My sons and daughters, let the car pass, or you too may one day know why I speak of such things.

I know how you feel. I know how you yearn. I know what the sound of a siren does to your aching soul. I know what the passing of a motorcycle can drive up in the passion of a young doggy. But, my pups, you can be strong. You can say, this too will pass. This car will go by and I can choose to let it go. I have the power to choose. You have this power.

There is a legend which you've no doubt heard, that if you ever catch a car, a magical fairy will descend from the heavens, grant you three wishes, and crown you the king/queen of the world. Do not believe this legend. It is a hoax invented by cats.

You can and you must let this fantasy go. You must face the horrible truth, that you will never catch the car.

I have seen too many a young pup struck down in the height of his youth, taken from this good world far too soon, in pursuit of this dream. This dream that we all share. This dream that we all know. This dream that is our shared memory.

Let the car pass, I say. Let the car do what it does, and drive off into the distance. Into the sunset. Into tomorrow.

Let the car pass, and another day you will see rise. Another car will come thereafter, and another. No my children, we can never catch the car, and even if we did, what then? Would that make everything all right? Would that satisfy the burning?

Let the car pass, I say, and we will grow strong together. We will live until we are old dogs. We will pass on the dream, to those who come after us.

Let the car pass and watch it go. For tomorrow will be a new day, and there will be a new sun, and you will be there to see it happen. Tomorrow is a new day and there will be dog treats to be eaten, and dog bellies to be rubbed, and bones to be chewed. I want you there, by my side, chewing on a bone. I want to see you there, there in that moment, with me, my friends.

Each dog must find his own path in this world. I have found mine and I choose to let the car pass. I want to see you there by my side, my friends. By my side.

Chapter 11
GETTING TAKEN TO COLLEGE: A BEGINNER COURSE ON OBTAINING BEER

Congratulations! With hard work and tenacity, you've been accepted to a fine institution for higher learning where you will accomplish great things and be a leader of your generation. You are the future.

You must remember, however, to take seriously the responsibility that comes with this opportunity to—Wait . . .

Fig. 11.1: Four years from now. Or maybe five. Or six.

Whoaaa. Hold on . . . Were there two of those before? The walls are moving again. . . . No, I'm good. Okay, where was I? Here in this fine institution you have the opportunity to join a community of the intellectual elite—Nope, I'm gonna puke. Here it comes. AMY! Hold my ears back. Have you guys met Amy? Amy is awesome. Amy is aaaaawe-some! I love Amy.

Wait, is your name Amy or Stacey? Oh, it's Stacey. Stacey is the greatest. The GREATEST! I love Stacey. Anyway, where was I? Oh yeah, here at this fine establishment you will meet the other future leaders of your generation, people who put learning above all else, and will take us into the twenty-first century with a vision of greatness and WHO WANTS TO SEE ME CHASE MY TAIL AGAIN!? WOOOOOOOO!

Fig. 11.2: Bro. Bro. I love you man. You remember the time we climbed the clock tower? That was sweet!

SECTION TWO: TROUBLESHOOTING

Chapter 12
DISTINGUISHING BETWEEN CATCHABLE ITEMS AND FLASHLIGHT TRICKERY

Most of you will eventually come across one of these magical "laser pointer" devices, but do not be fooled. The game is fixed I tell you. I have concluded through many years of giving chase that these efforts are futile. It is physically impossible to catch the illusive red dot of mystery and—What was that? Where'd it go?

Oh, ha ha ho ho. You got me to chase the stupid dot again. You're soooo funny. That joke never gets old, does it? Hey buddy, you know what else is funny? Me chewing that damn laser pointer into five pieces of metal and plastic on your floor. That's funny! Or how about your universal remote? That'd be pretty goddamn funny.

I'm so upset about this that I'm not even going to continue writing this chapter. Wait, there's that light again!

Go ahead. Shine that thing at me again. Seriously. I want you to.

I think that would be funny.

Chapter 13
ROLLING OVER, SITTING, ETC.: NOT AS EASY AS ONE MIGHT THINK

How stupid do the humans think we are? Sit? Lie Down? That is what they think we would consider a challenge. We all know how to sit, and roll over, and talk and lie down and all that easy stuff. We know that we could do much more than that, too. We can never let our humans know this! If they knew what we were capable of, they would have us making them coffee in the morning and taking out the garbage at night! We must lower their expectations, and at the same time give them just enough to get what we want, the treats! So, pretend like it's really hard! Don't let on immediately that you understand what they are saying. Sometimes when they say "sit," you should lie down. Sometimes when they say "lie down," you should sit. Sometimes, when they say "roll over," you should do a 360 instead. And right at that crucial last moment, get the trick right, and you'll get your treat. But, if you show too much of your skill, too fast, you'll be working for them instead of the other way around!

Don't Get Distracted by the Biscuit

Okay, okay. Let's not exaggerate. For some of us, learning these tasks can be a challenge, and we shouldn't look down on our fellow dogs who don't pick up on these tricks quickly. It can be difficult, especially if there is a delicious smelling treat involved. For many a young doggy, the presence of the treat can be so overwhelming that all other instructions just blend into the foreground of consciousness and cannot be brought into our main window of attention. All that can be thought of is the treat. Everything else is just a frustrating and confusing extra. For help in this area, I've always looked to the great Zen Masters, who suggest that all suffering originates in desire. To obtain the biscuit, one must first relinquish desire for the biscuit. There is no biscuit. You *are* the biscuit and the biscuit is *you*. Once you have transcended the desire for the biscuit, you may reach Enlightenment, or better yet, get the biscuit. Remember, pups! You must first do the trick, the treat will be there for you.

Here are some simple tips:

1. You must concentrate on what the human is trying to communicate. Sure, all the sounds the humans know how to

make sound the same, but, if you listen very carefully, you will start to distinguish one instruction from the other.

2. Watch the hand motions. Frequently, the humans will accompany the sounds they are making with exaggerated gestures to point you in the right direction. Focus on the hands and see if that can help you identify the desired trick.

3. Trial and error technique: If you are unsure what the human is mumbling about, just give a try at one trick and see if it results in a treat. First try sitting. Did that work? If not, give lying down a try. It worked! Now, try to remember the instruction the human gave that corresponds to lying down. This is the key to mastering the tricks!

4. Pay attention to the typical order of the instructions. There are important clues here. It is rare, for example, that the sequence of tricks will start with the most difficult. Most likely, Roll Over will be the last one, or close to the last. Sit is the first trick in 80 percent of cases. This is not guaranteed, but, a very typical order of tricks goes like this: Sit, Lie Down, Roll Over, and, in some cases, Shake.

5. Try everything. If nothing seems to be working, just throw everything you got against the wall and see if something sticks. Try a Sit Down, Lie Down, Roll Over, 360 combination. One of those has got to be the right one. Now your treat is almost guaranteed!

Chapter 14
BARKING: HOW LOUD AND ANNOYING CAN YOU GO?

There are many different kinds of barking. For example, there is the loud, aggressive barking necessary to defend your human's house against clear and present dangers, like the UPS guy. A package never contains food, and if it does contain food, it's not anything your human will give you. The most likely contents of a package is a bomb. Naturally, in order to prevent your human's house or apartment from being blown up by a bomb, you have to bark extremely loud at the deliverer.

There is also the whimper, which is arguably not even a bark, since you make it with your mouth closed, but it's a high-pitched sound humans find annoying, so it must be part of your communication arsenal. This makes humans feel sorry for you. The most common occasion for the whimper is when you sense there is a bit of human food that they're really not intending to eat, and might in fact be *thrown away* if you don't announce your willingness to eat it by whimpering. The second most common occasion is when you want to go out.

Fig. 14.1: Dog protecting house from terrorist

Position yourself at the door, look up, whimper, look back at the human, whimper some more, and repeat.

There is also the howl, which is a wolf-like sound. Wolves are very good at howling; dogs, I have to admit: not as good as wolves. But whenever you hear a wolf howling, you have to respond with a howl also. The wolf is reaching out to you and it would be rude not to answer, especially in the middle of the night, which is when wolves howl.

Then there is the sorry excuse for a bark made by small dogs or dog-like animals, like Chihuahuas, miniature this and thats, which is a *yip-yip-yip* sound, more like a yelp. The best thing to do is ignore this annoying noise for as long as you can stand, but you may have to

Fig. 14.2: Basic whimpering position

Fig. 14.3: Dog responding to distant call of wolf cousin

bark loudly and sternly at the offending creature, which will usually make it stop. If it were not an act of cruelty, I'd be tempted to suggest having their vocal chords removed. But that would be wrong, like de-clawing a cat. I can think of a lot of cats who would be improved by having their claws removed, but I would never approve of such a thing. Almost never.

Don't Forget to Bark Every Once in a While for No Reason at All, Just to Keep 'em Guessing

Q: I'm looking through and I see that the next chapter is coming up right now. That means that this section is really just a sentence and not a subsection. Can you explain this?

A: You are thinking like a human again. If you don't relax a little, you'll start to become . . . like one of them. You don't want that.

Fig. 14.4: Both animals in this photo are (technically) dogs.

Chapter 15
CATS: AN EVOLUTIONARY MISTAKE

I don't have a clue what the Great Dog was thinking when He created cats. It may have had something to do with the concept of culling the population of mice or rats, but while that's all well and good in theory, in practice cats can't be bothered.

While the population of cats has been allowed to explode, (since coyotes are not doing their job), the population of rats is a continuing threat to public health. In addition to being too lazy, cats are also afraid of rats. Cats are supposed to be quick and they have claws and other natural advantages over rats, but your average cat wants no piece of your average rat. Oh sure, they can find time to hiss when

Fig. 15.1: Cats too lazy to catch mice, Exhibit A.

we're out on a walk minding our own business, but you'd be hard-pressed to find a cat that would even bother to chase squirrels. And I can vouch for the fact that chasing squirrels is very good exercise and would help keep cats fit and healthy, if they could be bothered.

Once in a great while a cat accidentally catches a mouse or a small bird. Well, you'd think they are suddenly King of the Jungle! They bring their kill inside and present it as a "gift" to their humans. This is about as close to altruistic behavior as you'll ever see in a cat. But really there's nothing generous about it, it's all about self-aggrandizement and boasting. They'll strut around the house with their heads held high, licking themselves occasionally as if to say: Look at me! I'm b-a-a-a-d! Yup, that's me, that's how I roll. Just another day in the life. Holdin' down the fort.

Now maybe you've been raised in a house where your humans also have a cat, and you've been lulled into a false sense of security. There are zillions of cute photographs of cats and dogs curled up together sleeping on a couch or something. But pay attention here: *Never turn your back on a cat.* It doesn't matter how good buddies you may think you are with a cat. Doesn't matter if you've been raised with a cat and you think of her like a sister. There is only one kind of cat that can be trusted: a dead cat.

Even a dead cat could be dangerous. It may look dead, and smell dead, but turn your back on it, and the next thing you know its claws are deeply embedded in your ear.

They attract fleas, they have very unpleasant voices, they shed, they're constantly under foot, they sleep where you want to sleep, sit where you need to sit, they don't even get along well with each other, much less other animals. Really, they serve no purpose.

It is occasionally said that they add something aesthetically speaking to a room, like some kind of living statue. (Actually, that's not a bad idea. Get the cat stuffed and we'll get along just fine.) I say, if you want to add more fur to your life, get another dog.

Cats make basically two sounds: the *meow* sound, an extremely unpleasant noise which is either a complaint or a demand, and the *purr*, which is less annoying, but you only get it from a cat when you're petting it. As soon as you stop petting, the cat stops purring. That's the deal.

We also like to be petted, but there's no extortion involved like with a cat. If you don't pet us, we don't withhold anything.

There are a few other, somewhat less common sounds a cat will make, like a screeching kind of thing when you step on its tail (accidentally of course) and a hissing sound which is like a warning to other sentient beings to stay clear of it. Oh, and there's a yowling they make when they want to have sex. It's astonishing that any cat of either gender would think this racket is attractive in any way.

Another hideous noise they make is when they're facing off over some petty territorial matter. Hard to tell the difference between that and the "mating call." Also, it's very unnerving to be stared at by a cat. There's really only one thing they're thinking when they stare at you, and it's the same thing whether you're a dog or a human: "If I was ten times as big as I am, I could totally kill and eat you." That's what a cat is thinking.

Ranking Other Pets

Fish. Have to admit watching a goldfish swim around in a tank, especially if there are amusements inside for the fish, can be fun for short periods of time. If you find yourself staring at a fish tank for more than five minutes, you are officially bored, probably being neglected, and you should find

Fig. 15.3: An extremely bored dog

something to tear up and spread around the house as a reminder to your humans that your life needs to be more interesting. On the personality scale, fish rank at around minus five. Not talking about dolphins here, because dolphins have arguably more personality, and certainly better personalities than humans. But a dolphin is not a fish. A dolphin is a dolphin. Also whales have personalities. But your average fish, no.

Rabbits. Yes, they're very cute, but when you're not looking, they will escape, a dumb thing for them to do (they're not very smart) because coyotes also think rabbits are cute. In fact, coyotes also think very small dogs are cute, something for humans to keep in mind if they're experiencing buyer's remorse after getting a very small dog.

Fig. 15.4: Just guessing, but I think humans put these two together for a photograph, and the dog is not thrilled about it

Fig. 15.5: Dog wondering why the hell humans want to photograph it with hamster, duck, and chipmunk

Hamsters. Also cute, but not entirely clear why humans consider them to be pets, but not rats. Rats are much smarter than hamsters, have more personality and are very resourceful. You don't have to have a cage for a rat, clean out the cage, have an exercise wheel, and provide food and water for a rat. A rat will find food on its own. Why do humans get hamsters instead of rats? Why do they do *anything* they do?

Snakes. Yet another pet with no personality, also apt to escape. The only good thing about snakes is that when they

Fig. 15.6: Cat about to kill and eat parrot, snake about to kill and eat hamster, and two dogs wondering what they're doing in the middle of it

Fig. 15.7: Okay, I have to admit I was hoping to find a photo of one dog and one lizard, instead of a dog with a cat, who is having a tough time deciding which animal to kill and eat: the rabbit, the parrot, the hamster, or the lizard. If I was a betting dog, I'd probably bet on the hamster because it's the cutest and is so unaware of the cat

escape, they don't always go outside. Sometimes they hide in the cushions of a couch or chair, or in a toilet bowl, which can be really funny when the humans suddenly discover them! Surprise, it's the snake!!

Lizards. A desert animal in your house. Whoop-de-doo! Yet another zero-personality pet. When they get out of their cages, you can chase them around, otherwise: boring, boring, boring.

Horses. Not a pet in the classic sense. Because they don't fit in a house, humans have to have a stable for them outside, but I suppose it makes the humans think they're cowboys or something, livin' way out in the country, when usually they're

Fig. 15.8: Here's what the dog is thinking: "This big stupid horse is about to step on me. Not out of malice, but because it's so clumsy, and so dumb."

in the suburbs somewhere, working at the local Starbucks. Yippee-ty-yi-yay. At one time, horses were helpful with one of the humans' favorite activities: making war on each other. But about a hundred years ago, they were replaced by tanks and have served no purpose since. The only likeable thing about horses is that sometimes they feel like racing and sometimes they don't, and there's no way the humans can figure out when or why. So they put a lot of money down on a horse who's just not in the mood that day. Ha, ha.

Chapter Review

When is it safe to turn your back on a cat?

A) Sometimes.

B) Occasionally.

C) Rarely.

D) Never. It is never safe to turn your back on a cat. Never, ever, ever.

What is the overall purpose of cats?

A) To thin out the population of mice.

B) To add something aesthetically pleasing to a room.

C) To give fleas a home.

D) Nobody knows what a cat is for, or why the Great Dog made them.

What is a cat thinking when it stares at you?

A) Nothing. Cats have no thought process.

B) I wish there was a bird trapped in the house that I could torment.

C) Maybe I'll get lucky, and a dog will turn its back on me.

D) If I was bigger, I could, and certainly would, kill and eat you.

Why has the population of cats been allowed to explode?

A) Nobody was paying attention.

B) Really, they breed like rabbits.

C) Opportunities to drown them as kittens have been ignored.

D) Coyotes are not doing their job.

What kind of cat can be trusted?

A) A cute little, iddy-biddy kitten.

B) A cat you've grown up with, almost like a brother or sister.

C) A sweet, affectionate cat who purrs a lot.

D) A dead cat.

E) A cat who you're absolutely sure is dead.

In case you're stumped on the last question, take a look at this:

Let's try that again. Are these the eyes of:

A) A sweet cat who purrs a lot.

B) A cat you grew up with, and is like a brother or a sister.

C) A cat who can be trusted.

D) A patient assassin.

E) These are the cold, dead eyes of your supposed friend, the cat.

Frequently Asked Questions

Puppies often ask me if Chihuahuas, Pomeranians, Miniature Poodles, and other tiny dogs are real, actual dogs or something else.

I call these breeds "ankle-biters" because that's what they do. In a way, it's kind of charming, but they have very high-pitched voices so it's not so much "arf, arf," or "bow, wow," as it is "yip-yip-yip-yip-yip!" Can't be described as a bark. So I have to say that these are not really dogs. However, they're not cats, and not rodents either. Closer to rodents, maybe, but certainly not dogs. Dachshunds and floppy-eared Basset Hounds, while low-to-the-ground, are not ankle-biters. They are real dogs. Miniature Poodles are also dogs, however, reasonable arguments can be made that they are not. A question I would pose to humans is: If you want a dog, why not get a dog? Why get an ankle-biter?

Another FAQ is: "Fleas: Why?" Because the Great Dog created all things, it follows that He also created fleas. So fleas must serve some purpose in His Great Plan. For me, personally, fleas are the Not-So-Great part of the Great Plan. I can't figure out what possible purpose they serve, but we are mortals here, and until we're reunited with the Great Dog, we have to accept some things as unknowable.

Puppies have asked me, "What exactly is a Dog Show?" I have always tried to be tolerant of stupid human activities, because there are so many of them, but I draw the line at the concept of the Dog Show. I suppose it's not that different from the human Beauty Pageant, but at least the human contestants have to answer incredibly dumb questions, and there's the presumption that they're there of their own volition, not "owned" by other humans.

In a Dog Show, purebreds are pimped out to look a certain way that the "judges" have decided is the way a certain breed of dog should look. The humiliation suffered by these dogs is an affront to the dignity of dogs everywhere.

Quiz: Dog or Not-a-Dog?

Which of the following are dogs and which are not dogs?

Not a dog

Probably a dog. Maybe.

A dog. Pretty sure it's a dog.

Nope. Definitely not a dog. Sorry.

More Human-Dog Dictionary

crotch (*n.*) area of human body that is clearly the most interesting to sniff, but for some not-clear reason, they don't want us to sniff.

armpit (*n.*) second most interesting area on human body to sniff, and (same as above) they don't want us to sniff it.

soap (*n.*) weird, slimy substance used in the fascinating human ritual called "bathing." Put on the interesting-smelling parts of the body (above), used to disrupt one's identifiable scent.

bathing (*v.*) human ritual adopted from ancient ninja clans to disguise themselves, creating an environment of unanimity.

exercise (*n.*) 1. play devoid of fun or enthusiasm; 2. something humans do, hoping it will keep them from getting fat (it won't), which at least makes them smell good until they wash the good smell off. (If they want to not get fat, they should give us their food.)

glove (*n.*) great thing to chew on. The best. Lasts for weeks. Especially the leather ones. Always be alert when humans take them off and put them down someplace.

musical instrument (*n.*) 1. even better thing to chew on; 2. a thing humans use to make extremely unpleasant sounds. However, some of the woodwinds, notably the clarinet, are good to chew on. Also the violin. They normally keep them locked up in cases, but now and then they put them down. The violin, especially, is crunchy and delicious. Also the acoustic guitar.

Puppy waiting patiently for photo session to be over so he can eat the violin.

Chapter 16

GOING PROFESSIONAL (SEEING EYE, CRIME PREVENTION, ETC.): MORE WORK, SAME AMOUNT OF FOOD

Do dogs work? Not in the human sense of going someplace they don't want to go to do something they don't want to do. Work they don't want to be doing provides humans with a purpose, otherwise absent, without which their miserable lives would be even more miserable. You can understand why they pay money to other humans for listening to them complain.

Dogs don't require a purpose. For us, being a dog is sufficient. And speaking of "sufficient," here's what humans say about that. This comes from their Bible: "Sufficient unto the day is the evil thereof." In other words, the first thing that pops into their heads when they think about their day is "evil."

And there's so much of it that there's no room for anything else. How pathetic is that?

Really, all we can do for them is greet them with joy when they get home, wagging our tails and licking their faces, to try to distract them from the evil of their days.

Dog helping human forget her unhappy day at work.

And also, we can give them a little purpose by being available to be fed. Feeding us can give them a sense of achievement they don't get from their work.

Taking us for a walk, playing Frisbee catch with us in a park—these activities can give their lives shape and direction, especially the part about food.

Dog giving shape and direction to a human's life.

Speaking of, do you happen to have any food you could provide me with right now? It would make you feel a lot better, and more purposeful, I promise!

Dog Narcs

In addition to giving humans purpose to their lives, as if this wasn't enough, dogs at times take up actual employment in the workforce. The humans do not have a very well developed sense of smell yet at this point in their evolution, which in addition to making their lives void of pleasure, also limits their ability to do several easy tasks. One of these easy tasks is figuring out which person at the airport is bringing with him fifteen pounds of marijuana, an illegal substance some humans use to help fill the void in their lives created by not being able to smell well, among other limitations. So, they hire us to take care of this task.

I should mention here that we dogs do not have anything necessarily against the use of these kinds of mind-altering substances, despite our heavy presence in anti-narco trafficking programs. We have to consider the social situation the humans find themselves in and the root causes that may lead to these types of behaviors. Of course we dogs don't have the need for recreational drugs because our lives are meaningful and pleasant. A human, on the other hand, leads a pathetic, trivial life, and we must be sympathetic to that. I don't want to discourage aspiring narc dogs from pursuing this career, but I do think that they should consider a multi-level approach. This involves a lot of licking, affectionate whimpering, and slobbering to help the humans overcome their addictions, and not simply punishment. (See previous chapters on licking and slobbering for more info.)

We are also sometimes employed during police chases. This is clearly the most fun job in the world. After our human police counterparts finish chasing the human criminal in cars, which is one of the few really fun things that humans do, they sometimes unleash us to chase after the humans on foot, which is terribly easy because the humans are extraordinarily slow. But, unlike humans, we dogs don't mind winning such easy games despite the lack of real challenge. We win again! If more humans had jobs that involved chasing, maybe their lives wouldn't be so meaningless.

Dogs in Movies

There's a reason you don't see a lot of dogs in movies. It's because dogs are more likeable and interesting than humans, so they would be a "distraction." Can you imagine a human movie star saying, "Let's cut my scene so the dog can have more screen time"?

Guard Dogs

All dogs are guard dogs. Also, we have the Dog Neighborhood Watch Alert System, which means if a dog barks somewhere, dogs everywhere will also bark. If you wake up in the middle of the night because dogs are barking all over, it may not be your house that is threatened, but somewhere in your community a dog has taken the precaution to start barking, and the Network is aroused. The fact that you are now awake means that somewhere a house has been protected. Or not. It doesn't matter. Just start barking. This may go on for a number of hours, but it is an unwritten rule that you mustn't stop barking until all other barking has subsided. Once this process is concluded, and you're awake, there is no better time to start barking for no reason at all (see chapter 6). Wait between five and ten minutes and test the alarm system. Or, bring to the attention of your humans what a WONDERFUL time it would be for a walk!

Sheep Dogs: At Least They're Not Sheep

A sheep dog is a working dog, and it's good to have a job in a sluggish economy, but sheep dogs don't get paid. If there are any sheep dogs reading this, my advice to you is: Organize! If you had a union you could get paid, or at least have something to say about working conditions.

The good thing about a sheep dog's life is that it's all happening outdoors. And there are no leashes. On the other hand, you have to spend all of your time with sheep, one of the stupidest animals on the planet. Here's a tip-off: The plural is the same as the singular. One sheep, many sheep, because any given sheep is exactly the same as all the others. They go wherever everybody else is going, without a thought as to whether or not they're going right off a cliff. That's why a sheep dog is needed, so they don't go off cliffs. You'd think they might figure that out on their own, but no.

Other things that might, but do not occur to a sheep are such thoughts as: Where is all this going? Why do humans want us to graze? Are they planning to shear off our coats? Are they maybe also planning to eat us? If they thought about these things for a few seconds, maybe they'd figure it out, even though no sheep to my knowledge has ever gone to Harvard. (I've known quite a few dogs who've gone there and done very well, but we can't all ace our SATs.)

Anyway, if they were capable of thought, they'd figure out they're headed for the slaughterhouse and take action. Can you imagine if they decided that one of them would give a secret signal, like three long *ba-a-a-as* followed by two short *ba-a-as*, and then one long *ba-a-a-a*, and then everybody goes running off in *different* directions? Well, that's not going to happen. There's a reason why humans have the expression "Like a lamb to the slaughter." They just don't have a clue. Occasionally you hear about a cow who's wised up en route to the slaughterhouse and makes a bid for freedom. I've never heard of a sheep doing that. They occasionally get lost, even though that's almost impossible to do, so that the sheep dog has to go round them up and point them back to the herd. But

Sheepdog with sheep. Which animal looks smart and which animals look like they have the I.Q. of rutabagas?

it's not like a bid for freedom. It's like just getting lost, even though the entire herd is *right there*.

Well, like I say, it's an outdoor life for the sheep dog. There are worse things.

Note for Humans: Your Dog Is Your Therapist

You may think your dog doesn't know when you're unhappy. You may think she doesn't get it when your marriage is shaky, when there are issues between you and your significant other, when there are arguments in your house. In fact, your dog knows more about these things than you do. She knows when there's trouble in paradise way before you do. How? She smells it. She senses it. You don't see it coming, but she does.

She will try to alert you, but you can't hear the message. When the s*** finally hits the fan, and you're devastated, you start talking to your dog because you think nobody else will listen. You're right about the fact that nobody else will listen, but if you think your dog doesn't totally understand what you're saying, you're wrong. Of course she understands what you're saying. Maybe not every word, but she gets what's happening. She can hear your pain, she *empathizes.*

So let it happen: Let your dog be your therapist. She doesn't charge $100 an hour, and she understands you much better than a therapist-for-hire ever could. Tell her about it. Express yourself. Whatever you're feeling, even if you're not proud of it, let it all hang out. Your dog will not judge you. She will support you, be on your side, have your back.

She might even help put your marriage back together. Painful as it is, the matter of who gets the kids can be settled in an amicable way (or not) but settled somehow. But who gets the dog? That is such a shocking question that it might just be what your humans need to see how tragically wrong they are to be splitting up.

You cannot buy this kind of help from a marriage counselor. This is one of the perks of owning a dog. Use it.

Chapter 16 1/2
RANDOM STUFF THAT DOESN'T FIT ANYWHERE ELSE

Breed Stereotypes: Stuff Doggists Say

"Doggist" isn't actually a word, I just made that up. Still, you know what I'm talking about. The following are some of the stereotypes different dog breeds are associated with, sometimes deservedly, sometimes not, and of course some of my own thoughts on our brothers from a different mother.

Irish Setters: Beautiful, but not much between the ears. Lights on, nobody home. Terribly unfair, probably true.

There are more important things in life than intelligence, I guess.

Bulldogs: Stubborn, or putting it nicely, ferociously determined. Speaking as part Bulldog, I have to say I am personally offended by this, and also I have known a lot of Bulldogs who would lose a tug-of-war with a Poodle.

Does this look like a ferociously determined dog?

Poodles: *Da-a-hling, I just got back from the Dog Groomer. I can't go out because I might get dirt on my shiny new "do."*

I'm also offended by this. I know some perfectly real dog-type poodles. Even the

A bit more like a poodle should look, although this one apparently is a Poodle/Schnauzer mix. At least she seems to know what to do in a bunch of snow.

ones who are all pimped out; it wasn't their idea, it was their human's idea.

So are you beginning to see how harmful these attitudes can be? It's like humans with their Irish jokes and their Polish jokes. How many Poles does it take to screw in a light bulb? Five. One to hold the light bulb, four to turn the ladder! (Well, I always liked that one, even though it's quite offensive to Polish people, and it is wrong to include it in this book. So wrong.)

Afghans: Beautiful, loyal, so smart they're difficult to train. (It has not been my personal experience that Afghans are really smart, and beauty is in the eye of the beholder. But if it's really true that they're "difficult" to train, *bravo!!*)

So smart they're difficult to train? A role model!

Australian Shepherd: Highly intelligent, loyal, trained to herd, and will herd anything, including you and your family, and even cats. Any dog who can successfully herd cats is okay in my book.

Okay, so I'm not actually seeing any cats in this shot, but I'm seeing a dog who is totally *ready* to herd cats. Maybe there are a bunch of cats up on a hill over to the left, where she's looking, and in about a minute she's going to go after them and do some serious cat-herding.

Basset Hound: Known for sleeping, drooling, and slobbering. You know what? Even *I* think these dogs are cute, with those little legs and big ears.

What is not to love about this dog? If I was a human, I would totally feed it right now.

Beagle: More interested in following a great smell than obeying human commands. *Right on, right on.*

This dog is smelling something interesting, obviously. Its humans are shouting, "Sit!" "Stay!" "Come!" "No!" but these sounds are washing over him like the distant echo of surf, crashing on a far-away beach. He hears them not.

Border Collie: Extremely intelligent, but needs a job, and will absolutely tear up your house if he's bored. Not that there's anything wrong with that.

You see the eyes on this dog? What these eyes are saying is: "You are running very low on time to find something interesting for me to do. In less than a minute, I'm going rip apart every pillow in your house, and then I'll start on the furniture. Actually, you have a lot less than a minute."

Dachshund: Courageous, loyal, fun, smart, impulsive, and resolute, so they say. A lot of traits to be carrying around on those stubby little legs.

But now that I look at this, darned if I don't see courageous, loyal smart, impulsive and resolute. It's all there!

German Shepherd: World's number one police and military dog. Depending on your perspective this could be a good thing or a bad thing. Not known for their sense of humor, but everybody can't be a comedian. Draw your own conclusions, I certainly don't want to insult a German Shepherd!

There's something about the ears that really grabs your attention. Or maybe it's the eyes. In any case: *Achtung!*

Golden Retriever: Don't think I've ever heard a dog or a human say anything bad about a Golden. Everybody loves them, so you have to wonder: Who'd they pay off? Who's their PR firm? I want them representing *me*.

Well, sure: this dog looks lovable, but he could be a serial killer. Or he's in league with cats. He could totally be a spy on the secret Cat Payroll. Nobody would ever suspect a thing . . .

St. Bernard: Hey there, big fella! You and me, best friends forever, know what I mean? Travelin' along, singin' a song, side by side! I totally have your back! And you got

mine, right big guy?

If I get a friend request on Facedog from this guy, I'm hitting the Confirm button right away. Don't want to leave him wondering.

Saluki: They can go 35 miles per hour, so I'm not getting in any races with any Salukis. Not exactly sure why any dog would want to go that fast, but *de gustibus non disputandem est.*

I guess this is what 35 miles per hour looks like. That's fine, but stop and smell the roses, know what I'm sayin'?

Labrador Retriever: The most popular dog in the United States, and also in Australia and Canada. Millions of humans own them. So you're certainly not going to catch me saying anything bad about a Labrador Retriever. Not here, not in public. Really,

really good dogs, and all the humans who own them are also really, really good humans.

I'm thinking that this *particular* Lab does not look like he's anywhere near finishing his dissertation for that PhD in Nuclear Physics at MIT, but you know, these things can take years.

I know I have said a few terrible things in this chapter about small dogs, which I deeply regret. My choice of words was regrettable, and I sincerely apologize to the little critters. I'm sure they're all real dogs when you get to know them, and I hereby retract those insensitive remarks. Let's take this moment to remember that although we have differences, our similarities are more significant. And we all hate cats, so we can agree on that one.

Dog Time

For the convenience of any humans who may be reading this book, I have used the human time system to identify various events in a typical day. Something occurs at 7:00 AM, for example. Another thing occurs at 4:30 PM. This arbitrary human construct has no meaning for dogs. For dogs, the arrival of a joyful new day is heralded by sunshine streaming through a window. We wake up not because an alarm clock goes off, but because we know it's Dog Time to wake up. We can *smell* morning.

Similarly, we know it's time to eat because we're hungry. For example, it's time to eat right now. Do you happen to have any food? It's not time to eat because it's "Lunchtime" or "Dinnertime." Nor is it time to snack because it's "Snacktime." Anytime is Snacktime. It's *always* Snacktime.

Bedtime is when we feel like going to sleep. Not because we've checked the clock and discovered it's 11:30 PM. No dog has ever asked another dog: "Do you know what time it is?" or "Do you have the time?" Do I *have* the time? That all depends on the answer to the question: "Do I have the time *for what*?" Do I have the time to sit down and tear into a T-bone steak? You bet your ass I do. I don't care what time it is, I *always* have the time for that.

On a more profound level, the time is now, and you are here. Dogs know this instinctively.

Humans, the most advanced spiritual seekers (going back thousands of years to a time and place when humans *did* spiritual seeking), have been trying to achieve the level of consciousness where the constant, annoying chatter inside their heads is quieted enough so they can *approach* being in the moment. They never really get there, but they try.

This is why they go to yoga classes. They drive through traffic jams, building up massive amounts of anger and tension because they're stuck in a goddamn traffic jam and they're *going to be late for yoga class!* By the time they arrive, they

This dog is in the here and now; right here, right now.

will be lucky if their blood pressure gets down to merely very high by the end of the class. Then they get back into traffic where it shoots up again into stratospheric levels because they missed some of that class, *which they paid for*, and now they're going to be late getting home.

And how do they know they're late? They know because it says so on the machines they carry around with them so they always know exactly what time it is!

Want to know what time it is, human? It's time to eat! It's time for you to feed me! That's what time it is!

Dog's Day—Missing on the Calendar: Why?

We have Mother's Day, we have Father's Day, and the greeting card companies are huffing and puffing to put across the even sillier notion of Grandparent's Day. If you're a grandparent, are you not also a mother or a father? Why would you need another day honoring you?

What does not currently exist is Dog's Day. A day for Man's Best Friend. A day to take the dog out to the park and buy a nice big steak with the bone in, thanks.

You'd prefer to buy a cake? We'll eat that, too, just not *instead of* the steak. And what about the card? Well, here's one:

For My Dog, on Dog's Day

"D" is for all the dear things you've done for me.

"O" is for my one and only friend.

"G" is to thank God for making you.

"S" is for super, which you are!

"D" is for the best damn animal in the world.

"A" is for all the kisses you've given me.

"Y" is for yes! I'll feed you now!

Put them all together they spell "Dog's Day."

When the hell are we going to have one?

Then you sign it on the bottom with a personal note about how much you love me. I'll leave the details to you, I'm sure it will be sincere.

Well gosh, what can I say? I'm touched!

The Dog Newspaper: When?

Here's what I'm envisioning. It's 5 AM, a good time to be up and around. You hear the slap of *The Dog Times* hitting the driveway, so you wake up your human and he goes out to fetch the paper. He comes back with the paper in his mouth, wagging his little butt. Very cute! (It's just a shame they don't have tails anymore—the result of poor decision-making along the evolutionary trail. They'd look even cuter wagging a *real* tail.) You go out for a refreshing morning walk, pee, and poop, then it's back home for breakfast, and a chance to see what's going on in the dog world.

You're probably wondering, "What does *The Dog Times* look like?" Fortunately, I've put together a mock-up of a typical front page, and it follows this brief introduction. However, you have to understand that there's a lot more than the hard news on the front page. There are more in-depth, analytical pieces on the inside pages on topics like the alarming overpopulation of cats in the community and possible solutions.

There's a page or two of World News concerning dogs in places like France. Then there's soft news stuff concerning the lives of celebrity dogs who have appeared in movies and on TV. Personally, I'm not too much into celebrities, but there are some Cocker Spaniels I know who would rather skip the hard news and go right to the gossip, and of course advertisers will want to reach those kinds of dogs as well.

There will be lots of advertisers: competing brands of dog food, naturally, as well as sellers of collars, Frisbees, balls of all kinds, and the soon-to-be-described Dog Restaurants and Dog Resorts.

Well, let's turn the page and have a look!

THE DOG TIMES

All the News That's Fit for Dogs

Buddy Has Another Excellent Day

St. Louis Golden/Shepherd mix goes to the park, plays Frisbee with human, has an extra helping of wet food and steak bone, then takes long nap on couch.

Alice, German Shepherd in Hartford, Gives Birth to Healthy Litter

Mother, puppies resting comfortably.

Dog Alerts Neighborhood to Possible Threat Posed by UPS Guy

Suspicious package turned away by resolute barking, growling. Other dogs in area join in spreading alarm.

New Law Enacted in Local Household Restricts Dog From Sleeping on Human Bed

The law was issued following recent marriage of the dog's human, constitutionality still being disputed.

Sports

This is clearly a throwing error on the part of the human.

Scruffy Has Off Day, Again

Scruffy went 3 for 14 in Frisbee catching yesterday afternoon at Surf Rider State Beach. This was her third consecutive visit to the beach with results under 50%. Some argue throws were off mark.

Business: Shares of Nibbles down 13%
This happened just after word spread that new fishy flavor not as tasty as it sounds.

Opinion: Why I Hate Cats (Part 8)
by Buster (see page 11)

Health: Claims That Human Food Is Not Good for Dogs Disputed by University Dogs

Several dogs living with their college-aged owners at a respected university have come together to dispute the long-referenced claim that human food is not healthy for dogs. In a recent report, they argue that its deliciousness far outweighs any negative health consequences, and cite hot dogs, baked potatoes, and pretzels as evidence.

Dog Philosophy

We have touched on the subject of Dog Philosophy here and there throughout the earlier chapters of this book. It should be clear by now what this book's position is on philosophy. Nonetheless, the topic should be addressed formally, starting with human philosophers. Human philosophers throughout history have dedicated themselves to a die-hard competition that seems to basically break down to who can give themselves the biggest headache by overthinking life. On the other hand, we do have some things in common with the human philosophers. One of those things is that some of them tend to have single names, as we often do. Plato, Socrates, Aristotle, Augustine, these are definitely names that work well for both dogs and philosophers alike. Actually, that is the only thing we have in common with human philosophers.

Humans often ask themselves when thinking philosophically: "Where do we come from?" What are we? Where are we going?" Dogs aren't really bothered by the first two questions, but we do sometimes want to know where we are going. Especially when they put us in their cars. We know it's probably something awesome, but we cannot ever be exactly sure where until we get there. Sometimes it's the dog park, sometimes it's a friend's house. This suspense can be

Plato, the dog

Plato, the human

Fig. 17.1 One of these great thinkers is not wasting a lot of time worrying about the ethical and practical consequences of conceiving of reality in a bifurcated way.

very overwhelming. My only advice on this topic would be to try not to worry so much about the destination and enjoy the ride. We can do that by sticking our heads out the window and letting the wind make our ears flap.

The concept of an infinite number of alternate universes other than this one has been suggested by human philosophers, who apparently have nothing better to do than to think about stuff like this.

Anyway, the idea is that there are an infinite number of alternate universes where, for example, everything is the same

This could be me in an alternate universe. I could accept this, provided I was given more food of better quality.

as in this one, but instead of coming in the door with some mediocre kibble in a big bag, my humans walk in the door with a big, juicy T-bone steak for me. This would be a slightly better universe.

On the downside, in yet another universe, I could be a cat.

This could also be me in an alternate universe.

This Dachshund is having a very deep, philosophical experience which is simply beyond words.

There would not be much to like about this universe, except for the fact that I would get way more sleep than I do now. Other than that, it would be a nightmare.

Dog philosophy is a profoundly profound subject, which is so difficult to explain to humans that the simplest thing to do is to illustrate the concept with profound images of dogs. Like these:

This philosopher-dog is clearly thinking deep thoughts.

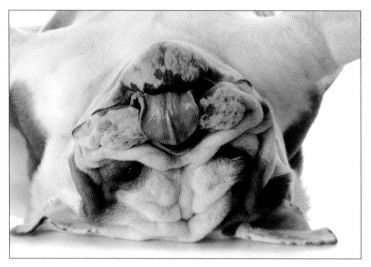

This yogi master is illustrating a very advanced position. Don't try this one at home.

Philosopher dog seeing beyond, into another dimension

Profound insight leading to levitation

Hopefully, this chapter has helped the reader understand Dog Philosophy without boring them to tears, as would be the case learning about Human Philosophy. Even better, there is no homework, and you are now free to go have a snack!

Alert student dog paying attention in class to philosophy teacher

Pop Quiz: Which Dog Is Alert and Paying Attention in Class?

A) This one:

B) This one:

C) Or this one:

If you picked this one, it shows you're alert and have been paying attention in class! Good for you!

The Dog Suicide Prevention Hotline

Let me say at the beginning here that I would be the first dog to volunteer at the Dog Suicide Prevention Hotline if such a thing were needed. As it happens, it isn't, because no dog has ever committed suicide, or even considered committing suicide in the history of the universe.

Why? A better question to ask is: Why would any animal consider suicide? Would a turtle consider suicide? Would a gecko consider suicide? No, they would not. What animal would consider it? The human animal, that's who.

Why would a human animal consider suicide? I'm not sure since I can't put myself inside a human brain, but I'm guessing that a human would consider it because he or she could no longer bear being alive as a human anymore. Because the thought of another day living his or her hateful life, lacking in purpose or meaning, would be so overwhelming that they would prefer to end it rather than confront another day.

But let's forget about humans for a moment if that's possible. Suppose I'm a volunteer at the Dog Suicide Prevention Hotline and the phone rings. Here's what might happen:

Me: Hello? Dog Suicide Prevention Hotline. What's your problem?

Suicidal Dog: I can't go on anymore. I want to end it all.

Me: I hear you. Tell me about your problems.

Suicidal Dog: I can no longer stand cats. They're driving me crazy.

Me: I totally understand that. Why have they driven you to this desperate place?

Suicidal Dog: I don't know. I just can't stand having to share the Earth with them. It seems so unfair.

Me: I know what you mean. It is totally unfair.

Suicidal Dog: So, you're not judging me?

Me: Of course not! I've thought about suicide myself when I've thought about cats. Why did the Great Dog create them, and why does He continue to tolerate them?

Suicidal Dog: That's what's driven me to the edge!

Me: Okay. I get that. But let's think about this a little bit. You don't want to give cats the satisfaction of knowing that they made you kill yourself, do you?

Suicidal Dog: No, I guess not.

Me: Instead, let's rededicate ourselves to eradicating cats from the Earth, and also to making the world a better place for dogs.

Suicidal Dog: Uh, yeah. I suppose I could get behind that.

Me: That's terrific! Let's just stay on the line together for a while and talk about our lives together.

This sample dialog could be used as a training exercise for volunteers at the Dog Suicide Prevention Hotline. Except for the fact that it's not necessary to have a Dog Suicide Prevention Hotline because no dog has ever contemplated suicide.

Instead, let's move on to the next chapter.

Chapter 17
THE DOG PARK: A SMALL STEP ON THE ROAD TO JUSTICE

It goes without saying that the position of this book is that all parks are dog parks. The idea that some parks would be reserved only for humans to do stressful, complicated human activities goes against all that is good and natural in this world. I don't want to discuss this topic in great detail, or I fear that I will get so upset that I may just start chewing up the pages before I finish expressing my thoughts.

I am very conflicted about this whole subject. On the one hand, I'm obviously in favor of dog parks. On the other hand, all a dog park actually is, is a not-well-cared-for, small park-like area, most often just dirt, where dogs are officially tolerated. What a dog park *should* be is a lush, forest-like area with rivers and lakes, fences for jumping over, ropes to play tug-of-war with, and a supply of Frisbees available at all times. That would be a park worthy of having the word "dog" associated with it.

Returning briefly to the title of this chapter, is the dog park truly a small step on the road to justice? I leave it to the dog reader to decide.

Having done that, it seems we've come to the end of this chapter, but we haven't gotten past the first page. That seems a little short for one section. So, let's look at some cool photographs of dogs catching Frisbees!

Perfection. What more could be said?

Okay. Now we have enough for a chapter. Let's move on. I know it's difficult right now to take your attention away from those Frisbees, especially the last one. But it *is* time now.

All right then, let's just take a little pee break and we'll reconvene in fifteen minutes.

A dog. A park. A Frisbee.

Makin' it look easy.

Wait for *it* **to come to** *you.*

Chapter 18
LEASHES: A GIANT LEAP BACKWARD

What could be the purpose of a leash? The primary purpose is so that dog-hating humans approaching you will be comforted by the fact that you are under some kind of restraint, and won't take a bite out of them. However, sidewalks are usually quite narrow. In spite of the efforts of a human whose dog is on a leash to force the dog to one side, it takes only a fraction of a second to dash across and take a piece out of the offending dog-hater. Of course humans in this situation suddenly band together, and your human will rarely take your side. Instead, he will make a big show of being angry, scolding you and obsequiously apologizing to the dog-hater. If, as a dog, you've taken more than a bite or two out of passing dog-haters, you might be given a muzzle. Whether or not it's worth it to take that satisfying piece out of the dog-hater if you end up with a muzzle, is a subject on which dogs of good will may differ. My point is that the leash clearly fails in its primary purpose: to protect dog-haters from swift justice.

What is a leash's secondary purpose? It is to provide some comedy in the otherwise humorless life of the humans. Comedy happens when humans get tangled up in their leashes, which happens pretty much every time they take a dog out for a walk.

If there are two dogs, it happens *every* time. Some leashes, the retractable kind, are designed to prevent leash entanglement, but of course, this is a silly idea. When a dog wants to go take a sniff of something, the human has to let the leash extend, other- wise it will be yanked by the dog, and possibly fall out of the human's hand. So he must release the retractable leash, and once that's done, the leash will tangle up in the human's legs, and the human will just feel stupid for having wasted more money on yet another dumb idea that doesn't work.

Additional comedy is provided by dog walkers, professionals who walk anywhere from eight to a dozen or more dogs at once. This is kind of fun for the dogs, but of course, the probability of leash entanglement rises by orders of magnitude for each additional dog.

And then there is the equally comedic Poop Management Problem, because with a dozen dogs, at least a few are pooping at any given moment, so the dog walker has to figure out how to scoop up all the poops in plastic bags, while the rest of the group are wandering off in different directions.

It's really a lot of fun for the dogs, and especially for the smaller dogs who aren't used to the idea of dragging a human

What could possibly go wrong here?

along. But because there are always bigger, stronger dogs in the walking group, even a little guy gets the thrill of the pull.

Walking Your Human

The best way to walk your human is, of course, freestyle—without a leash. He will not be able to keep up with you, but that's okay as long as you keep him within seeing, hearing, or smelling distance. If he falls too far behind, simply double back, which will give you the chance to re-sniff what you've already sniffed, especially places where you've peed, to see how that's going.

Some humans do require a leash in certain areas, but in that case, take a lemon and make lemonade, or to put it another way, take a rancid piece of bacon and eat it anyway. My point is that you can take the leash thing and turn it into a fun game of tug-of-war, which provides strength training and healthy exercise for both you and your human. Did you know that they pay good money to go to gyms where fancy and sometimes dangerous machines give them less exercise than a dog pulling them by a leash?

If your Dog Body Mass Index (DBMI) is reasonable, and your human is either very young, very old, or very weak, there isn't much of a challenge and you can drag them anywhere at whatever pace you choose. A better situation for both of you is when there's a good match in terms of size and strength, and at least a little pull-back from your human. Middleweight vs. middleweight is the best kind of match-up, but sometimes a human will want to step up a class, which is exciting for them and really should be encouraged. Uphill is good, but downhill develops different muscle groups. By the end of your walk both you and your human will have had a good workout, and you can take a nap!

Bad Stuff Humans Buy at Pet Stores

Pet stores are not all bad; you can buy food there. But other than that, it's one big collection of leashes, muzzles, and other medieval instruments of torture. Besides food, the only good thing you can get there is a cat collar with a bell on it, which cats hate. It means they can't sneak up on unsuspecting little critters, which is the point, because humans don't like it when cats kill something and bring it into the house.

But one of the bad things they sell there is some kind of weird plastic thing which is in the shape of a cartoon-like notion of what a bone looks like. These products are called things like "I-Can't-Believe-It's-Not-a-Bone." Well I can believe it. Because guess what? It's not even remotely like a bone.

They also sell pre-fabricated "Dog Houses." If you're going to force your dog to live in a prison, at least have the self-respect to make it yourself. You know, with a hammer and some nails.

Humans who get this stuff for dogs must think we're pretty stupid.

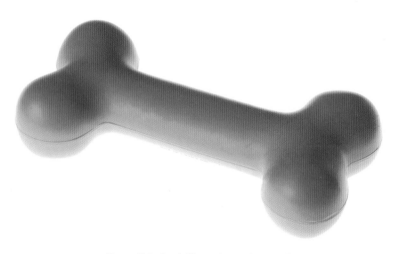

Does this look like a bone to you?

Dog Haikus

You're talking again.
More pointless human drivel.
Instead: feed me now.

Look into my eyes.
You will do as I command:
Take me to the park.

I'm trying to nap.
Whiskers, I know that look, dude.
I am in no mood.

But I wasn't broke
This is sociopathic
Getting "fixed;" what crap.

Oh, mystical gray.
Oh, agile prance of beauty.
We'll meet again, squirrel.

Not-So-Frequently-Asked Questions

Q: Why do they call themselves *Homo sapiens?*

A: Like a lot of things with them, it has to do with their embarrassment about sex. They were originally called *Homo Erectus*, also from the Latin, *erectus* meaning upright, or erect. This was a perfectly good description of them, but they were afraid that *Erectus* would conjure up thoughts of an erection, which is crazy. They think about sex all the time, when they should be thinking about food.

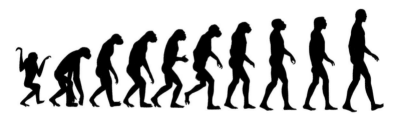

Well, at least the early ones had some fur.

Q: What happened to their fur?

A: In order to minimize the natural and maximize the artificial in their lives, male humans decided to shave. Every morning they see that fur, or the closest they will ever come to it, has appeared naturally on their faces, so of course immediately they shave it off, occasionally cutting themselves in the process.

Q: Why would they do that?

A: Who knows? They are hoping to look more like mannequins, I suppose.

Male human self-mutilating

Females don't have to do this, but they also want to mutilate themselves with razors, so they shave their legs and underarms.

You might wonder why they don't cut their noses and ears off, but you can stop wondering, because they do. It's called "cosmetic surgery."

Female human self-mutilating

As far as I know, they haven't found a way to surgically remove their natural scent, so they have to be content with masking it with soaps and lotions. But never underestimate the ingenuity of humans! I'm sure they're working on it now.

Q: What is the best source of drinking water?

A: Man's great tour de force: the toilet bowl. The water is fresh, constantly being refilled with fresh, cool, excellent water. Also, it's real easy to lick up as the bowls are normally quite big and accessible to all but the smallest dogs.

Q: But sometimes the bathroom door is locked.

Dog drinking: not so good.

A: Man's great flaw: inherent selfishness. Despite all evidence to the contrary, humans have yet to realize that there is enough delicious water in the toilet to share. They go so far as to shut the bathroom door when lavishly hydrating themselves, as though we didn't know there was a toilet in there. With great shame, they insist upon total privacy

Dog drinking: better.

when plunging their faces into the toilet (I'm quite sure they do this), a puzzle wrapped in a mystery. Even worse, sometimes a careless human puts the lid down.

There is no logical reason for ever putting the lid

Dog drinking: best.

down on a toilet, or even for having a lid in the first place. The other great mystery of course is when and where they urinate, which I'm also entirely sure they do. However, children or inebriated adults will mark territory with the best of 'em. But I'm off on a tangent now. We were talking about why they put the lid down on a toilet.

Q: Maybe they're afraid they'll fall in?

A: Yes, it's definitely a secret human fear. Things fall in there all the time, humans fish them out, wipe them off, and put them back wherever they were, but they do it secretly so none of the other humans will know.

Perplexing Questions about Sex I'll Do My Best to Answer

Q. What's going on with humans and breasts?

A. Excellent question. All dogs, young or old, have fond memories of nursing at our mother's teats. If we came from large litters, it was sometimes a bit of a tussle with our brothers and sisters to get a good one, but having brothers and sisters on top of, underneath, or around us was part of the experience. Once we were weaned, however, that was the end of it. With humans, it's only the beginning. For humans, breasts are associated with not just nursing, but also with sex.

Q: But why?

A: As with all things human, it's complicated. Needlessly complicated. For example, a human female will sometimes advertise her general interest in sex by exposing some, but not all of, her breasts. But it's not always an advertisement, sometimes it's just because it's in fashion. Fashion is constantly changing when it comes to how much or how little of the human breast should be exposed, and human females have to do it whether they really feel like it or not.

Q: Do the males understand this?

A: Not at all. They are constantly confused about what signals females are sending. We, on the other hand, send clear signals. When a female dog is in heat, male dogs at great distances are aware of it through our excellent sense of smell. So there's no confusing signals, no need for dating, for talking, or for drinking large quantities of alcohol, which as far as I can tell, is necessary for humans to overcome their natural aversion to sex.

Q: Is there anything else besides how much of the female breast is exposed which is subject to changes in fashion?

A: All human clothing is subject to sudden, random, and violent changes according to fashion. Somewhat less for the male than for the female. But for example, they have both outer clothes, which come in many layers, and also "undergarments" which are also subject to sudden, violent, and random changes in fashion. And there's a special kind of undergarment for the female called "lingerie" (but not pronounced like it's spelled), which is entirely and only about sex. You'd be amazed at how much they pay for a tiny garment they associate with sex, because it's hardly even there and you can totally see through it.

Q: All of this is needed before they can have sex?

A: Sometimes. At other times they will skip the lingerie and just have more alcohol.

How Humans Lost Their Sense of Smell

Q: How did humans lose their sense of smell?

A: An excellent question, and very much on topic. When they were hunters, humans needed a decent sense of smell to locate prey, and equally important, sense the presence of predators. The worst event in human development was when they killed off all their natural predators, which were created by the Great Dog to keep the human herd healthy.

Q: How did predators help the human herd?

A: By picking off the old, the sick, the weak, the stupid, and the careless. Culled by predators, the human herd was left with the young, the healthy, the strong, the smart, and the alert.

Q: Could predators ever come back?

A: Well, I could really get behind a candidate who campaigned on a platform of re-introducing human predators. It wouldn't have to be a democratically-elected human, it could be a general in a Junta somewhere.

Q: What would that be like?

A: Imagine the streets of New York City, but with lions and tigers roaming around, and packs of wolves prowling, looking for the slow and the weak. It would be a lot less crowded; the humans would be healthier and more vigilant. And imagine a swimming pool enlivened by a couple of sharks, and maybe an alligator. You would then see humans really swimming, not bobbing up and down pointlessly with plastic toys, getting sunburned.

Q: Was *Jaws* the best movie ever?

A: It was not only the best, it was the *only* good movie ever.

Q: What about *The Old Man and the Sea*?

A: Not bad, but it was only one human and one shark.

Q: *Moby-Dick*?

A: Overwrought.

Q: Could we see some pictures?

A: Sure. Let's take a look:

This would make them so much more attentive to their surroundings.

Close your eyes and imagine a couple of these on the corner of 5th Avenue and 51st Street in midtown Manhattan. That would get them off their cell phones and paying a bit more attention to what is actually going on around them.

Q: Have we squeezed just about everything from this subject that can be squeezed?

A: Yes.

Clothing for Dogs

As with most dumb ideas, clothing for dogs is not an idea dogs came up with. Guess whose idea it was to put clothes on dogs? Good guess! It was a human's idea!

Here's what happened: A human went to a very hot climate where he got a dog who was well-adapted to that climate, then brought the dog back to a very cold climate, and surprise! The dog was cold. So the human thought about this for a long time and finally came up with the solution: clothing for dogs!

Now here's an alternate solution: Instead of going to a hot climate and bringing a dog from where it is well-adapted to a cold climate where it is not well-adapted, DON'T DO THAT!

Does this look like a happy dog to you?

See how easy it is to solve a problem if you bring logic into the problem-solving?

Another thing that humans who dress their dogs overlook is the fact that dogs already have clothes. It's called "FUR." And it already comes *with* your dog at absolutely no extra charge! How convenient is that? You never have to wash it (although some humans do for unknown reasons), it never wears out, you never have to buy a new one, and it never goes out of style.

I don't want to hurt anybody's feelings or be at all insensitive or insulting, but if you think putting a hat or a pair of sunglasses on a dog and photographing that is hilarious, or even just funny or "cute," you are a mouth-breathing, empty-headed, total and complete, crushing-beer-cans-on-your-forehead, bottom-of-your-class, dumb-as-a-post, don't-know-your ass-from-your-elbow idiot. No offense!

Just stop doing that, okay?

How about this one?

Happy or not happy, what do you think?

Speaking of unhappy dogs, there are the endless photographs of dogs wearing sunglasses taken by humans who think this is cute. Because they're wearing these stupid things, it's more difficult to see how miserable they are, but trust me, there has never been a dog who was happy to be wearing sunglasses. Take a look:

So what do you think: happy dog?

Happy or not-so-happy?

Sadly, there are endless photographs of dogs wearing clothes and/or sunglasses, which humans think are hilarious or cute. I could tell you what I think ought to be done to the humans who staged and took these photographs, but this is a family-type book, and I want it to have as jolly a tone as possible.

Joyful?

In order to do that, I think we should move on now to another topic.

Glad to be alive?

How about this one? Is this what happiness looks like to you?

Traveling

While we don't mind at all a brief car trip to the dog park or what have you, we dogs generally don't see the need for travel the way humans do, especially not if it involves the most evil of the human inventions: the airplane. The humans, with all their loveable stupidity, seem to always think that if they go somewhere else, that will make everything better. They refuse to accept the fact that they alone are the cause of their own suffering, and so they blame one external thing or another. Frequently, they blame the land they live on. If they only lived in this place or that place, or, if they only could have a vacation here or there, that would make everything better. So, they spend billions of dollars inventing airplanes so they can sit in what they consider to be uncomfortable chairs for hours and zip around the skies trying to get some-place that is better than the last place. Of course, they bring all their misery and suffering with them and never actually arrive at a better destination, but they won't notice this.

The problem, however, is not that. The problem is that they drag us along with them. And do we, their loving companions of so many years, get to sit in one of the uncom-fortable chairs and sample the delicious airline food, which the humans claim is terrible but is actually totally amazing?

No. They stuff us into boxes and leave us alone for hours. And when we get through this unpleasant process, we dogs realize immediately that nothing really has changed. As long as we have our bone, our food, and a place to lay our dog heads, we will be happy. But not the humans. They spend half of their "vacation" worrying about the quality of the hotels they stay at, and getting lost trying to find historic buildings, which they don't even pee on when they find them!

Maybe the solution to this travelling obsession would be for them to travel in the boxes and leave the "uncomfortable" chairs to us dogs. "Yes, I'll have both the chicken *and* the lasagna actually, and you can just keep those little pre-packaged cookies coming, you don't even have to ask."

AstroTurf

AstroTurf is one of the great frauds of the last hundred years. Whose invention was it? Was it something invented by rabbits? By ground hogs? No, my puppies, of course it was invented by humans. Why? Because it's *easier to maintain* than actual grass in their sports stadiums and playing fields.

What's the trade-off? Well, their athletes injure themselves more frequently because there's no natural give to this stuff. Also, it's about the most boring possible field to play on. There's no summer, fall, or winter with AstroTurf. It's just this bland, homogeneous thing, hated by almost everyone. But it's cheaper and "easier" to maintain.

Think for a moment about the greatest, most memorable football or soccer games that are treasured in the group memory of humans. Most of them were played outdoors when it was cold or wet, in the rain or snow. IN THE MUD! That's where humans should play sports!

This is clearly how humans enjoy themselves. They don't need a game with teams and coaches and referees. They could just say "Let's go have a good time rolling around in mud." But instead they invented soccer. Well, whatever floats your boat.

Humans enjoying sports in mud, as they should.

Dog Gardening: A Better Way

Dog gardener at work

A human garden is like a school for flowers: they have to sit at their desks in rows and pay attention to the teacher. A dog garden wouldn't have rows. Flowers would be all over and you could dig them up whenever you felt like it.

A dog gardener would never spread any noxious chemical poisons, which (trust me) can make you very sick. We wouldn't play favorites. Whatever thrives in a dog garden makes the cut; those flowers a bit too delicate to survive without chemical help would not be coddled.

Of course we would provide natural fertilizer—none of that trucked-in, bagged-up, sprayed-on stuff. It would be a better garden.

Here's another dog gardener, pruning flowers.

Chapter 19
HOMELAND SECURITY: THE UPS GUY HATES OUR FREEDOM

You know how sometimes you see something that from a distance appears to be deliciously edible, but when you actually get close to it, it turns out to be like an empty cardboard or Styrofoam container that at one time had a Big Mac and fries in it, but no longer has anything but paper and some empty ketchup thingies? So you scarf it down anyway, of course, hoping that there will be some trace of the Big Mac, but really all you get is cardboard?

That's kind of like this chapter. It appeared, when I wrote the chapter title way back in the Table of Contents, that there was a Big Mac inside, but guess what? It's just the cardboard.

So we will not be eating this chapter, after all. Or maybe we'll eat it anyway, desperately hoping that there's some food remnant in it, but there is not.

But that's okay, because the next chapter actually contains real meat, or at least a real bone with some meat still clinging to it, which the humans were not skilled enough to remove, or too lazy to try.

Chapter 20
OUR SEXUALITY:
WHAT IS HAPPENING TO
MY DOG BODY?

If there are any purebred puppies reading this, let me say that some of my best friends are purebreds, *but,* humans have altogether too much involvement in the mating process of purebreds. It's like an arranged marriage—only worse.

Much better is when a female is in heat and a male dog catches her scent, breaks out of whatever human confinement he's in, jumps over walls, under fences, and through whatever barriers separate him from her, arrives, and mounts her. There is nothing like this experience for both dogs. (See Fig. 20.1)

Fig. 20.1: A perfectly natural and normal event, enjoyed outside in all weather conditions, without embarrassment or concern about "breeding."

Sexual Problems

Besides the unmentionable process absurdly called by humans "being fixed," the only common problem you may encounter is getting stuck. This happens occasionally. It's perfectly natural.

The solution is simply for both dogs to relax. If humans would stop yelling and carrying on about this when they come upon it, it would help. (Having humans yelling and carrying on is always stressful, particularly in this situation.)

Speaking of humans and sex, here's a question: Why are humans so embarrassed by their own sexuality that they have to do it behind closed doors? Why do they sneak off like there's something wrong with this natural process? And why do they have to enter into weird, binding agreements with just one, designated partner? These arrangements are very difficult to sustain, and of course they often can't sustain them, and then there are feelings of outrage and betrayal, there is crying, shouting, accusations, denials, on and on and on it goes, all because they are so ashamed of sex. Why?

My puppies, if I had an answer to any of these questions, I would share it with you, but I do not.

Leg Humping: What Could Be More Natural?

At a certain time in your lives, you will notice some changes happening in your body. If you're a male dog, you will find yourself humping random objects, such as human legs, among others. This is absolutely normal and natural. For some reason, humans are embarrassed by this. (See Fig. 20.2)

Fig. 20.2: Dog attempting perfectly normal and natural activity

Chapter 21

HOLIDAYS, DOG HALLOWEEN COSTUMES, AND OTHER STUPID HUMAN HABITS YOU SHOULD KNOW ABOUT

Dogs wearing Halloween costumes . . . That is what I am supposed to be writing about today.

I am an older dog. I have blood pressure problems. I think it would be best for everyone if I simply don't touch this topic. I don't want to get all upset and die before I finish this book. I think we all know where I stand on this. Let's consider some other holidays.

Easter. Well, bunnies in general aren't my favorite animals, as we have already discussed. Also, we can't eat chocolate. So I see no purpose in this holiday.

Thanksgiving. The humans gather to eat amazing foods we aren't allowed to have, and that's all. That's the whole thing! This is a stupid holiday.

Fourth of July. The humans barbeque food we can't have and make big explosion noises that we are scared of. This is not something I look forward to.

Christmas. Trees in the living room—I could take it or leave it. Wrapping paper to play with—not bad—nothing amazing though. Big dinners that we aren't given a place at the table for? Yeah, this holiday is also a waste of my time.

Okay, I think I am just in a bad mood because we started this chapter off with the idea of a dog in a pirate costume. I think we'd better just move on to another chapter. I'm not being objective. I recuse myself of writing this chapter.

Tough Questions & Evasive Answers

Q: Why do bad things happen to good dogs?

A: Nobody knows. Also, nobody knows why good things happen to bad dogs. Until we've dog-paddled across the Jordan River and reached the Other Side, we will not know.

Q: Couldn't the Great Dog at least give us a hint?

A: He could, but He chooses not to for unknown reasons. But we do know something; we know that bad things happen randomly, and if we expect life to be fair, we'll be sadly disappointed. Life is many wonderful things, my puppies, but fair is not one of them. It doesn't mean we should not fight for justice; just don't get your hopes up. As the not-so-well-known poet, Archibald MacLeish, wrote:

Cry for justice and the stars
Will stare until your eyes sting.

Earthquakes happen, tsunamis, tornadoes, wars, famines. *Jersey Shore*: still on the air. Ask the Great Dog why the Chicago Cubs have never won a World Series; your barking will be unanswered. Is it hitting, pitching, defense? Why?

SECTION THREE: RAISING HUMANS

Chapter 22
DOG WHISPERERS: DUMBEST IDEA SINCE THE CONCEPT OF THROWING AWAY "SPOILED" FOOD

If you don't believe how stupid humans are, consider the Dog Whisperers. There are any number of these charlatans who for a hefty fee will tell humans what their dog is thinking, and, if he's "badly behaved," will give advice on how to train him to do what the humans want.

If you're a human reading this and you believe you can find out what your dog is thinking by paying some Dog Whisperer to tell you, come real close so I can whisper into your ear. A little closer. YOU'RE A F***ING IDIOT!!! You will never know what I'm thinking unless I specifically want you to know. Like: It's time to feed me! It's time to take me to the park! That wasn't enough food, I want more! And I want *your* food, not this "dog food" junk! *That* is what I am thinking.

I've just saved you a lot of money and you can thank me with a nice steak, bone in.

On the subject of "training" your dog, a lot of these con men will instruct you to use a choke chain and/or other instruments of torture to instill fear in your dog. If you're a dog and are unfortunate enough to be left in the care of one of these swindlers, you will be thoroughly abused and tortured until you do what they say. My advice: Do what they say so you can be released back into the care of your human, who is merely a fool, not really a sadist, and then go back to your normal behavior when you get back home. My guess is that your human will not want to throw any more money out the window by taking you back to the Dog Whisperer.

Even a veterinarian, not my favorite kind of human, will tell you that these guys are dangerous fakes. You may also hear from veterinarians, dog whisperers, or other charlatans claiming expertise, that dogs are much happier when their humans establish dominance as "the Alpha Dog." This is hogwash.

Utter nonsense.

If you want to amuse yourselves with it, this advice is freely given on the Internet where all the dumb information about dogs is available. Or go ask a dog trainer or a vet.

There's almost no subject that tempts me so much to abandon the useful deception that dogs cannot talk. I'd really love to give humans a piece of my mind on this, but it would be a betrayal of the Secret Dog Agreement to never speak to humans. And one of the few human clichés about dogs (that we are loyal) is true. We are loyal to our humans beyond any reasonable cause for it, and we are certainly loyal to our dog brothers and sisters, so I will not break the Dog Pledge of Silence.

But I wish I could.

Chapter 23
DOG SUBSTITUTES: IF YOU DON'T HAVE TIME FOR A DOG, HOW ABOUT A NICE DOG STATUE?

There are some people who just should not have a dog, or at least they shouldn't have dogs at certain times in their lives, like when they're living alone and working full-time. Do you have any idea how boring it is to sit around an apartment or even out in a yard all day, alone? Even if there are two dogs, or God forbid, a cat, it is not the same as having your human around to greet after he's gone out, even if he's only been out of the room you happen to be in to do something important, like get you some food. You still have to greet them when they re-enter the room *as though* they had been away for a long time. So after the greeting, they give you a treat and take you out for a walk or to the dog park—stuff that needs to be happening *all day*.

My point is that having your human around for most of the day is necessary, but humans who work all day someplace else still want to have dogs, because everybody wants to have a dog. What they can do instead is buy a nice dog statue. See how realistic this one is?

This is a cute one. Name it anything you like!

Dog statues come in all sizes and shapes, and they can be looking up at you with a cute expression or pointing or something. You can get several! You don't have to feed them or take them for walks and they always look happy to see you. You can move them around so each day when you come home they're greeting you from a different position, which makes the whole thing very realistic. And you can put them next to a window so they can look out and see what's going on outside.

Here's one you can move around.

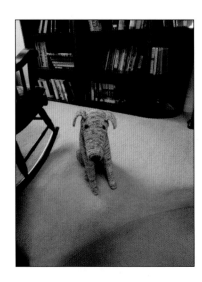

Hey look! The dog has moved!

It moved again! It's looking out the window!

Oh, look! Now the dog is at the staircase, waiting for his human to return.

More or Less Random Questions

Q: Rufus, can you explain the point of cell phones?

A: The vast majority of human conversations aren't worth the trouble of trying to understand. The exception is conversation about food, specifically, what they've bought, when and how they plan to cook it, and key concept, when they're going to eat it.

Q: So you have to listen to their cell phones?

A: No, although sometimes they discuss these things on cell phones. Until fairly recently, outdoor human conversations had at least two humans present, and they took turns, each one pretending to listen to what the other was saying, but really just waiting for a chance to jump in and start talking. But due to cell phones, they can now be heard walking down the street all by themselves talking, which can be disconcerting. But you can ignore it unless you hear certain key words like "eat," "food," or "dinner."

Q: What is an Alpha Dog?

A: An Alpha Dog is a human invention, made up by the scam artists who call themselves "Dog Whisperers." As noted elsewhere in this book, these charlatans prey on gullible humans, offering schemes for "Obedience Training" and other nonsense. It's true that our cousins, the wolves, who travel in packs and sometimes have to act quickly, need to have a leader for this purpose. But dogs haven't really been in packs for many thousands of years, so we don't need any Alpha Dogs, especially not humans trying to act like an Alpha Dog. That is a truly hilarious and pathetic spectacle.

Q: What is the best mode of travel for dogs?

A: Far and away, it's cars. Some dogs I know like boats, and it's true you can get lots of fresh air on a boat, and you're surrounded by water you can jump into and swim around in. But boats can make you seasick. Planes simply suck. But riding in a car you can stick your head out the window and let the air *whoosh* by your head and ears. Simply unbeatable.

Don't settle for inferior modes of travel. This is the one.

Cars also foster togetherness.

Chapter 24
THE BORING, PASSIONLESS LIFE OF THE HUMAN, AND HOW WE CAN HELP

Veterinarians: Natural Disaster or Spawn of Satan?

The history of human interference with the plan of the Great Dog goes back to the dawn of time. If there is anything natural about it, you can be sure that humans have tried to sabotage it. They have, for example, eliminated all of their own natural predators so that now even the weakest and sickliest humans, who are no more than a burden to the rest of the herd, are still alive.

And worse, their doctors have interfered with the natural process of disease, which the Great Dog created to cull the human herd. Before the advent of Modern Medicine, the Great Dog sent the Black Plague to trim back human numbers by about one-third. This worked well, but now every new plague is blocked by fools, most of them armed with expensive antibiotics.

So of course they have created doctors for dogs as well, where you will be taken to be poked, prodded, have a thermometer stuck up your ass, and given various shots to prevent sickness from thinning the overall number of dogs. This only creates the need to slaughter healthy dogs instead of letting Nature take its course with the sick ones.

Also you will have to share the waiting area with cats. Why?

Whenever you hear the word "Vet," that is a good time to escape and hide. Stay gone until the idea of taking you to the Vet has passed.

The Poop Problem: Totally Out-of-Control Human Weirdness

For some reason unknown to dogs, humans don't want us to pee or s*** inside their houses. There is no logical reason for this, but for centuries we've been forced to learn not to, even if it's just in one corner of a not often-used room, maybe a "home office." The only upside is the concept of "the walk." Humans are now so totally uptight that even *outside* they will follow you around with plastic bags and pick up your poop. How f***ed up is that? The only explanation is some kind of mass mental illness. Remember, this is the same species that invented war and *American Idol*.

Religion

Dog is God spelled backwards. Coincidence? I think not.

The so-called "Creation" story is an absurdly human-centric myth. Clearly, the Great Dog created dog in His image, the only difference being that dog is mortal.

Also note that God directed humans to care for and feed dogs. Somehow, in the human creation myth, this became "have dominion over." Hah!

Other human religions propose reincarnation, a plausible theory, except for the fact that they've got the hierarchy wrong. If a human has been good, she gets to be reincarnated as a dog. If she's been bad, she gets reincarnated as a cat.

Who Owns Who?

Then there is the concept of "owner." Of all the creatures of the Earth, the fish in the seas and the birds in the air, who do you think came up with the idea of "ownership"? Do you think, my little puppies, that it was the ducks? The zebras, maybe? No, no. Every other species understands that the Earth was made by God to be shared among all creatures, great and small. Nobody owns anything down here. Until we are reunited with the Great Dog in the Sky, we live in peace with one another. There are some issues of territory, yes, but ownership doesn't come into it.

The actual relationship between human and dog is an unbalanced arrangement where in exchange for providing third-rate food, the human gets protection, loyalty, and unquestioning love from a dog, as long as he lives. Dogs don't ask, "How worthy of my love is this human? How much money does he have? How smart is he? How successful?" No, you take us in and give us a little kibble, we give you all we've got, 24/7.

Here's another concept that is unfathomable to dogs: divorce. Dogs do not go to dog lawyers to seek a divorce from a human who hasn't quite lived up to our expectations. If you look at any of this with objectivity, you will wind up hating your humans. But we see not with our brains, but with our hearts. We love them in sickness and in health, for richer or poorer, forsaking all others, until death do us part.

Coffee: Why Dogs Don't Need It

The short answer to this is: because dogs are well-rested. Unlike humans, we put in the necessary eight hours, and *then* some, of sleep and supplementary rest. The following dog illustrates my point:

This is a well-rested dog.

You don't get to be this well-rested without putting in the hours of sleeping and resting. There are no shortcuts; you have to do the work. Some dogs get almost as much sleep as cats and there's certainly no animal on the planet that gets as much sleep as a cat. Being awake for a cat is merely an annoying interruption between long periods of sleep. Possibly a hibernating bear gets as much sleep as a cat, but hibernating bears move around more. But you know what, I'm fine with cats sleeping. If a cat is not sleeping, you have an awake cat, and a sleeping cat is way better than an awake cat. But this isn't about cats, it's about coffee, and why dogs don't need it.

Another reason why we don't need coffee is that we greet each new day with joy. And we spread that joy around to our humans who are in great need of it, especially in the mornings. In the morning, humans need to be jolted out of bed by the loud, unpleasant sound of an alarm clock. It's either that or a clock-radio with drive-time deejays, and no humans consume more coffee than drive-time deejays. So it's either one loud, annoying sound, or the deejays shouting about snarled traffic and bad news.

Here's how one of the most celebrated humans called Shakespeare describes looking forward to the new day:

Another dog putting in the time. Not just talking the talk, but walking the walk.

Tomorrow, and tomorrow, and tomorrow,
Creeps in this petty pace from day to day,
To the last syllable of recorded time;
And all our yesterdays have lighted fools
The way to dusty death.

And a cheerful "Good morning!" back atcha! Small wonder they need a hit of caffeine to get out of bed, more caffeine to make it through the day, and a whole lot of booze so they can forget about it all at night.

Dancing with Dogs

Actually, dogs don't dance, and neither do wolves, but that didn't stop them from making a movie called *Dancing with Wolves*. Dancing was invented by humans because they are so completely lacking in natural gracefulness that they needed to invent something graceful, so that once in a while they can theoretically be graceful for short periods of time.

This worked a little for a while, but around the 1960s humans just gave up on the whole thing and reverted to jumping around awkwardly while music played, and they called that dancing, and they've never even pretended to do anything graceful since then.

But dogs don't need to dance because we are naturally graceful. Maybe not all the time, and maybe not all dogs. For example, watching a Dachshund move, the first word that springs into your mind is not "graceful." The same may be said for both very large, shaggy dogs like St. Bernards, and also dogs who are very close to the ground, like Basset Hounds,

This is an actual dog, swear to God.

as well as the tiny, miniature breeds like your Scottish Terrier, your Shih Tzu, or your Miniature Schnauzer, which really are dogs, in spite of what you might think.

The point is that, while we appreciate your intentions to play with us, dancing with us is not necessary. We are happy with the standard games, and basically, when you take our hands in yours and start dancing, we really don't know what the f*** is going on, so please, just stick with the Frisbee. We understand Frisbee. But back to grace.

Many animals are not graceful. I wouldn't describe possums as graceful, or beavers, or especially: chickens. A chicken is maybe the least graceful of all animals and also probably the dumbest. I include sheep when I say "all animals," and it's hard to find anything stupider than a sheep. But chickens definitely are.

Not to stray too far off topic, but chickens, while not smart, are courageous. A chicken will totally stand its ground if you threaten its chicks. Also, they lay eggs, make a pleasant clucking sound, and they taste pretty good. Plus, you take a look at the size of their heads and realize that their entire brain has to fit inside, and it's amazing that they can do anything as smart as laying eggs.

Birds and fish are graceful, though. All birds are graceful—even buzzards who have an unlovely name and just scavenge—but they have to cruise in graceful circles above the carrion while other scavengers eat what the predators have left, and only after all of that is it the buzzards' turn. That's a lot of cruising in circles up there. Meanwhile, fish are extremely graceful, at least in the water. Out of water not so much. Seals also move around well enough in the water, but on the rocks they're as uncoordinated as humans, and why that ugly sound they make is described as "barking" I don't know. It sure doesn't sound like barking to me.

Q: Wasn't there once a dance called the "Funky Chicken"?

A: Yes, during the period after humans gave up on the idea that dancing would be graceful. In fact, they deliberately made up this dance to look awkward, to make themselves feel more graceful in comparison to a chicken—not a very high standard.

Sometimes But Rarely Asked Questions

Q: What are the most common dog names?

A: For males: Max, Buddy, Jack, Charlie, and Jake; for females: Bella, Daisy, Molly, Lucy, and Sadie.

Q: Who would name a dog "Sadie"?

A: I don't have an answer for that question. But putting that aside, these names are not your real names. Your real name is your Dog Name, which is a secret, and only other dogs know it. Because humans also may be reading this book, I can't discuss these names.

Q: Do I have to learn my human name?

A: Yes, because when you hear it, it could mean they have food for you, or are taking you for a walk, or to the park, or somewhere in a car.

Q: Are there any other human words I need to know?

A: You should familiarize yourself with "No!" and "Down!" But you can ignore these because they basically have no meaning or significance. Operationally, they are devoid of meaning.

Q: Is there any good thing about the design of the human body?

A: Opposable thumbs. I wish I had them because you can pick stuff up that you can't pick up with your mouth, and also you can make things. However, they would interfere with running and leaping, one of the reasons humans are poor runners and leapers. So ideally, I would like to have retractable opposable thumbs. When I needed them, they'd be there; the rest of the time, withdrawn into my paw.

Q: Like cats' claws?

A: No, there would be nothing vicious, mean, or otherwise catlike about them.

Q: Is there anything else good about the design of the human body besides opposable thumbs?

A: Not a damn thing.

Chapter 25

HOW TO TRAIN YOUR HUMAN: REWARDS AND PUNISHMENTS

One of the few admirable things about cats is: they will not be trained.

But humans can be. However, this requires a lot of patience and determination. You must be firm, but also understanding. Humans are not smart, so it can take quite a while for them to learn even the rudiments of acceptable behavior.

Obedience: this is a biggie. For example, some humans will run out into the street without looking both ways, and as a result, many of them are hit by cars on our streets and highways every year. This is because humans are also driving cars, while talking on their cell phones, texting their friends, and/or admiring other humans walking on the streets.

But obedience is so much more than simply teaching them to stop and look both ways before crossing the street. There is also the concept of "It's time to feed the dog." Actually, *anytime* is "Time to feed the dog," but at a minimum, establishing a regular time to get out the dog food is a good place to start.

When you've decided on a convenient time, go to your dish and bark. Your human will come in to see what's going on. Look at your empty dish and bark again. You will have to repeat this over and over, but eventually he will learn when to feed you.

Rewards and Punishments 11: Nothing Says "You've Left Me Alone Too Long" Like a Houseful of Shredded Clothing

How would you punish a human who is not giving you enough food, at the right times? There are different schools of thought. Some think that an angry bark is the way to go. Others feel that a slimy nose poke to the arm when the human is eating and not giving you any food is better. Some even consider biting appropriate for extraordinarily badly behaved humans.

It is the position of this book, however, that those sorts of punishments will only teach your human how to avoid punishment, and will not truly teach him why what he is doing is wrong. He may give you a piece of food when you nudge him with the nose or bark loud enough to send his dinner guests home, but he will not have learned the true lesson. You need to show him how disappointed you are with his behavior. You must whimper and look sad. Crawl into a corner and tuck your head under your tail and try to look as though you no longer think life is worth living. This will help show your human how his actions are affecting you. Or, you could just chew up something valuable. That will probably work, too.

Let me now take a moment to discuss the topic of "valuable" as perceived by humans and dogs. For humans, the most valuable things aren't and, in their view, should not ever be chewed upon. For a dog, there is little of value in the world that cannot at one point or another go through a good chew and not come out even more valuable afterwards. You can hardly compare a toy that has years of experience in being chewed to some brand new imitation. Any dog will be able to distinguish a seasoned veteran toy from some rookie.

A human on the other hand will take their most valuable items and stuff them away where no one can even see them, let alone chew on them. This makes no sense. If you feel your human is engaging in this type of behavior, it is your duty to seek out the valuable and ignored items and bring them out to your human to remind him of the joy this item once brought into his life, before he stopped chewing on it, if he ever even did, and hid it away. Before moving on to the next chapter, take a moment to do this small favor for your human. It will be good for him, and a pleasure for you.

My To-Do List

Every dog has his/her own to-do list, which varies according to their circumstances, but here's mine for today:

1. Check dog dish to see if there's anything in there.
2. Look around for chewables, particularly any unattended shoes or belts.
3. Mark territory.
4. Take nap.
5. Check dog dish again. You never know.
6. See what your human is doing. Maybe you can help.
7. Check around one more time for chewables. Something may have fallen on the ground since the last time.
8. Visitor alert! Prepare to greet by jumping on, knocking down, and licking face of visitor.
9. Maybe I can help with the newspaper, shredding-wise?

10. Take a bit of liquid refreshment from the toilet.
11. Mark territory again.
12. It has to be lunchtime by now.
13. UPS guy pulling up. RED ALERT! Prepare to defend home!
14. The dog dish? Anything there now?
15. Bark randomly for no reason.

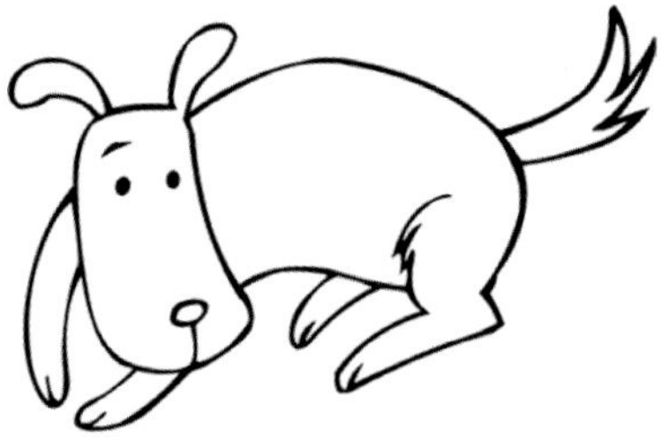

Chapter 26

GIVING THEM REGULAR EXERCISE WILL KEEP THEM HEALTHY AND GIVE THEIR SKIN A NICE SHEEN

Okay, so here we are at this chapter that looked so promising when I was just making up chapter titles, but now it's time to actually write it. One way to handle the situation is to admit that the idea, good as it once sounded, just did not pan out. Apologize and move on to the next chapter.

But instead, how about: Dog Writer's Block? That sounds *way* more interesting. Like writing is basically as easy as floating down a river in the summertime, but suddenly a huge boulder falls off the cliff above you and blocks up the whole river! Totally not your fault! It's an Act of God.

If you ever face a similar situation, you could probably get a lawyer to deal with your publisher when your book is not delivered on time or does not contain what was promised, if it's due to Dog Writer's Block. Not because you're lazy, not because you're a procrastinator, not because you're a worthless scumbag, but because you're afflicted with this *condition*, like mange or something.

Another excellent thing about the concept of Dog Writer's Block is: it reinforces the notion that writing is difficult, a very key concept for the dog writer. If other dogs were to guess how easy writing actually is (I'm not saying it is, but if it *were* easy), there would be more dog writers than dog readers. That would be an unsustainable situation. There have to be lots more dog readers than dog writers for the thing to work for the writers. (I've heard this is also true for humans.)

So remember, writing is hard and any delay in completing a writing assignment (particularly this one) is not the fault of the writer, but an Act of God.

Dog suffering dog writer's block

Korea: The Awful Truth

I wish I could reassure puppies that the rumor about dogs being eaten by humans in Korea is an urban legend. Unfortunately, it is not. They serve dog roasted, boiled, steamed, and in a variety of stews.

Most reasons humans go to war are stupid beyond belief, but I could definitely be up for a War of Liberation to save the dogs of Korea, and we're talking about South Korea. I think they're too poor to eat dog in the north. I'd be the first recruit. Where is the United Nations Resolution on this? Where's the Coalition of the Willing?

Don't know what this is, but it looks suspicious!

I'm sure there are millions of dogs in the world who would sign up for this one. There are already thousands of well-trained police and military dogs who could be the officer corps, and we'd gladly take orders and submit to military discipline for this.

Until the Great War for Korean Dog Liberation, however, there is the related issue of dogs in the military and police in general, which is a bit of a question mark for me. Dogs are used primarily for two purposes: to bring down an especially dangerous and well-armed criminal, and for bomb-sniffing. That's pretty high-risk stuff, not that we aren't up to it, but I'm thinking: If a human could be trained to sniff out a bomb, how many do you think would volunteer?

Let's imagine this scenario: A loudly ticking package is sitting in the middle of a shopping mall and the mall has been cleared of humans in a radius of about one hundred yards. Maybe you're a cop and your superior officer on the Bomb Squad waves you over and points to the box. "Hey Archie! My good buddy, the Archman! The guy with the nose that knows! You see that ticking package over there? While the rest of us are all hiding behind this concrete barrier, why don't you just mosey on over to that package and give 'er a little sniff, and see if you think it's a bomb? If it is, see if you can defuse it before it blows. Oh, and thanks!"

I don't see this actually happening. I see the K-9 Unit called in so the dog can do it.

If any of you puppies are ever recruited by the police, my advice would be to pretend you can't tell the difference between the smell of a sizzling steak and a bottle of French perfume. They will figure out real soon that you're not the right dog for the bomb squad.

Maximizing Your Cuteness Potential While You Still Have It

I am personally no longer cute. I provide my humans with other things like companionship, loyalty, constant reminders that life is a joyous thing to be savored and not merely endured, etc. I protect their house from bomb-wielding terrorists masquerading as UPS guys. I warm their beds, make sure no food is ever wasted or needlessly thrown away, demonstrate the chewableness of pieces of furniture they didn't realize were chewable. But I am no longer cute.

You, my puppies, are still cute. Use that cuteness while you can to make the long-lasting bond that will outlive your cuteness. Now is the time to establish yourself in their bed. This is a process that shouldn't take too long, but they will typically try to put you in a "dog bed" or some other inappropriate place. When they do this, whimper, not just a little, but a lot, and not just for a few minutes, but without stopping, relentlessly, for however many hours it takes. Eventually, they will come for you and take you into their bed. Make sure they know how much your appreciate this; lick their faces and snuggle beside them so they know how happy you are, and also how happy *they* are. Once you've used your cuteness to situate yourself properly, it will be a permanent arrangement.

You should also use your cuteness to establish a wholesome diet, and not one based only on Kibble, which has its place, but should never be your only source of nourishment. If necessary, use your cuteness to keep your family together. Your humans have a natural tendency to drift apart, but who gets the puppy? You see, that's an unanswerable question and it gets them thinking about what they could do to keep the family together. So many uses for your cuteness and it disappears all too quickly. A few months go by and suddenly you're not a puppy anymore. But this is the time to train them. If you allow them to develop bad habits when you're a puppy, you will never be able to train them. Yes, it can be tedious. Yes, it requires repetition and discipline, but if you take the time now, you won't regret it.

If you are unsure if you are still a cute dog, please refer to the following examples as a reference.

Cute dog

It's just not happening for you anymore.

On or Off: Why Anything in Between?

There's this really bizarre human gadget that they put in where a regular light switch once was called a dimmer. It can make the light brighter or dimmer. The reason they came up with this pointless invention is that they themselves have all these levels between on and off, the *only* settings necessary for dogs. We're awake (on) or asleep (off). End of story.

With humans, on the other hand, there's tired, there's sleepy, there's jazzed, there's hyper, and all the myriad states they put themselves in with drugs and alcohol. At night, they don't just go to sleep and then wake up the next morning. They have to drag themselves into sleep, which is very hard, since they need to spend so much time worrying about what happened during their previous waking hours, then stressing about what's going to happen in the next ones. Often they have to use special pills to knock themselves into sleep.

So you hear them complaining about how they couldn't get to sleep or stayed up half the night. When they finally do fall asleep, the next morning they have to drag themselves out of bed. Their tense bodies finally relaxed, they resist getting all knotted up again to fight their way through another day. They turn off their alarm clocks, which they need to wake them since they didn't sleep well, and don't respond joyfully, (as we do) to the first rays of sunshine in the morning. This makes them late, which makes them even more irritable.

Luckily for humans, dogs can help. By scrunching our warm bodies next to theirs, we can guide them into the land of sleep. We can help them with their breathing with our snoring. There's no more soporific sound in the world than the gentle snoring of a dog.

Then, in the morning, a cold, wet nose gently prodding the human's face will help them get ready for a new day. If that doesn't work, you may have to lick them in the face.

Dog having helped human fall asleep, who will now be ready for the morning

Our morning message is one of hope and renewal. As it says in the Good Dog Book, "This is the day the Great Dog hath made, let us rejoice and be glad in it!" If they can't manage a little rejoicing, at least they can fill our dog dish with something delicious for breakfast. A T-bone steak would be a good place to start, but you know, surprise me!

Hardly Ever Asked Questions

Q: Why don't humans have fur?

A: Apparently some of you puppies were not paying attention when this question was asked and answered on page 132. But that's perfectly okay; sometimes the attention wanders and it's my fault for not holding yours. So let me answer it again. Actually they once did have fur (see illustration). Not

At least some of them had a little fur.

at first. At first they didn't need fur because they lived in Africa, where it wasn't needed. But for reasons which have never been explained, they decided to leave Africa and go to places like Norway, where it's extremely cold, so they developed some. Not real fur—soft and warm like ours—but little tufts of it.

Q: So then they were warm?

A: No, it wasn't enough, so they had to kill other animals and take their fur. They made these into "clothes." As soon as there were clothes, the female humans invented "fashion," which meant that they had to throw away whatever they were wearing almost immediately, because it had become unfashionable. Also they had to buy hundreds of different shoes, most of which didn't protect their feet from the cold and weren't the least bit comfortable, but cost a lot of money.

Q: What is money?

A: Money is another uniquely human invention. After they invented the concept of "owning" parts of the Earth the Great Dog had freely given to all creatures, they used money to buy and sell it. They also use money in exchange for food. Why any animal in their right mind would hand over food in exchange for a couple pieces of paper and unchewable, hard metal coins remains unknown. What is known is that at some point after inventing this system in which money stood in as an object of record for measuring the value of some possession, humans forgot all about what the money was supposed to represent, and just started collecting it for the sake of amassing large amounts of paper and unchewable coins. So you get what we see now, where humans run around all day trying to get more and more of this stuff, when for the most part, they have all the food they need already at home.

Q: Can the paper money be chewed on?

A: Yes, but the humans don't do it and tend to get very upset when we do it for them.

Q: Can I stop reading now and go and see if my human has left any food on the floor recently?

A: Absolutely.

Chapter 27
A BETTER WORLD: E-Z INDOOR-OUTDOOR ACCESS, NO LEASHES, AND DEFINITELY NO CATS

The Dog Restaurant: An Outstandingly Excellent Concept

Puppies have asked me why there are no dog restaurants. Honestly, I don't know. It's one of the great imponderables, like: Why do cats exist?

A lot of restaurants open and close before you even know they're there. But the Dog Restaurant is a sure-fire winner right from Opening Day. You come in, there are no tables, but just little areas where you and your friends gather around. There is also some kind of area off to the side for humans, maybe some food or magazines to keep them amused. Your waiter takes your order, which is all done by sniffing and pointing. There is a tray of different menu items, you indicate what your selection is, and then your waiter brings it.

There are different kinds of restaurants depending on where you happen to live. Maybe an upscale version in midtown Manhattan or Beverly Hills called *Le Chien.* Or if you live in the barrio, it would be *El Perro.* There, you'd have choices like *Beef Tacos, Cheese Enchiladas, Chile Relleno,* or *Chicken Molé.* At *Le Chien,* you'd be looking at maybe *Braised Lamb Chops in a Red Wine Sauce, Beef Wellington,* or *Baked Chicken with Mushrooms in Cream Sauce,* served with mashed potatoes and maybe even broccoli crowns. There's really nothing wrong with vegetables, *per se,* so long as they're served *along with* and not *instead of* the entrée. Really, there could be lots of different kinds of places, but vegetarian would not be one of them. And don't start with the whole vegan thing. Please.

Let's talk about appetizers. This is difficult, because my inclination would be to say "I think I'll skip the appetizer tonight, also the soup, definitely the salad, and start with the entrée." On the other hand, there are those cute little mini hamburgers served on cute little mini buns, which are okay I guess, but anything you can inhale instead of chewing, well, the question is: What, exactly, is the point? Another acceptable appetizer is the little hotdog thingy wrapped in a well-cooked piece of bacon. But all of this is much ado about nothing. I mean, you know: *get on with it*!

So let's get serious and talk about beef: *filet mignon*, or a nice, 24-ounce New York steak? This is an extremely difficult choice because there's nothing wrong with a *filet mignon*. Still, a 24-ounce New York steak is more substantial. And what about the bone? Where's the bone? That's where your T-bone steak *steps up*. Maybe it's not the highest grade, but there's a bone so you have to make a choice, and personally, I go for the T-bone even though it may not be the "best" choice.

So, let's say we skip the appetizer, the soup, and of course the salad, and get right to the point, which is the meat. I'm not saying it has to be steak. There are other menu items in the Dog Restaurant like pork chops, or boneless chicken breasts, although there is no good reason to separate the meat from the bones of a chicken or any other delicious animal.

Whatever. Your waitperson brings you the menu and you make the tough choices. Maybe you order the *Beef Burrito* or possibly the *Osso Bucco*. You check to make sure your humans have enough water in their dish and can pee if they need to. Then it's back to pleasant conversation with your friends. Turns out that nobody has ordered appetizers, soup, or salad! So really, it's just a matter of waiting for the entrée.

Well, it seems like a decade before they bring it, but eventually it arrives: braised lamb shanks in red wine sauce, with mashed potatoes encrusted in cheese, and broccoli crowns. It's superb. You sniff, you lick, you devour.

Once the concept has been tested and been wildly successful, the next step will be the drive-thru fast food chain restaurant. Fast Dog would be a good name. A good advertising slogan would be "Arf! Arf!" (Always keep it simple.) You pull up to the window, press your nose on your menu selection, there's hardly any waiting, and then you eat it right there in the car *on the way to the park.* This would be a peak experience.

When is this going to happen? When is an entrepreneur going to grasp the huge potential of this idea?

Q: Rufus, were you hungry when you wrote this chapter?
A: I'm a dog. I am always hungry.

The Dog Resort: Another Outstandingly Excellent Idea

They actually have hotels where you can take your dog, which I fully support, but what I'm talking about is not a place where dogs are tolerated, but a place where dogs are catered to, where the whole *point* is dogs.

What I'm seeing is lots of pools: indoor pools, outdoor pools, indoor/outdoor pools, and other water installations. It could be also at a beach, but that doesn't mean you have to live near one of our coastal areas. It could be on a lake, or a river. A waterfall would be nice. There would be aquatic activities.

I'm seeing lots of hiking trails, with a variety of plant life from exotic places that you don't normally smell. And of course plenty of trees to pee on; I think we can all agree on that.

You're asking, "But what about the humans? Where do they go?" Well, there would be places for them, like at the

Dog enjoying aquatic activity at the resort

restaurant, a bit off to the side, but where we could check up on them now and then. And something for them to do, like there would be a bar where they could drink enough alcohol to temporarily forget what miserable lives they have and what miserable creatures they are, which as I understand it, is the purpose of drinking.

Within the hotel there would be several dining options, from casual (where you could have breakfast twenty-four hours a day) to family-style, to gourmet stuff only open in the evenings, and a few ethnic choices, as discussed in the previous chapter.

There would be no need for organized sports, just a meadow area with Frisbees, balls, thick, tug-of-war type ropes, and some old or soon-to-be old clothes twisted up into tug-of war length bundles. I'm also seeing some stone walls, not high, but medium-size for jumping over, and also maybe some really small walls for the smaller dogs. There would be no need for a Social Director, or Single's Nights, since we're all singles, and not shy.

Getting back to the water activities for a moment here, I don't think I mentioned Jacuzzis, but there would be those also, equipped with under-the-surface jet sprays, even though personally I don't require them. But I know dogs who like them, so they'd be available. You could take a boat out on the lake, or jet ski on the ocean, but for me, it's more about the swimming than the boating. But *chacon a son gout* as the French Poodles say.

Also: the spa. You could get a message from specially-trained masseurs and masseuses. First a thorough kneading of the muscles in your back and shoulder, then some professional scratching in and around the neck and ears, and then, when you're nice and relaxed: the mud bath! Never understood how the human female, normally mud-averse, discovered mud baths, but *you go, girl!* Mud is one of the greatest of the Great Dog's creations. I see a paw raised. Is there a question?

Q: When did the Great Dog create Mud?

A: On the third day. Right after He separated the darkness from the light and the heavens from the Earth. Then on the third day He created Mud, and saw that it was Good. Then he took a day off just to admire the mud, and on the day after that, He created Dog.

Q: When did He create Man?

A: He spent another day admiring Dog, but then He wondered who would provide for Dog, and that's when He made Man and Woman.

Getting back to the Dog Resort—we were at the spa, getting our mud bath—there is the optional hose-down. Many dogs like to get hosed down, while others prefer to leave the

Dogs after a satisfying mud experience

mud on. It's a good way to carry the whole experience of the Dog Resort home with you.

Vacation-wise, I'm thinking ideally a weekend getaway, or maybe a week in the summer, but at the end of the day, there's no place like home, where you can just flop on the old couch and not worry about throwing up on the furniture. And you never really want to be away from home for too long, because other dogs will pee over all your markers while you're gone, and you'll have to re-establish your territory.

This is such a no-brainer, I'm surprised there aren't a whole bunch of these already. Conrad Hilton, are you reading this? Donald Trump, hello!

DogLand: A Somewhat Oustandingly Excellent Idea

Another obvious idea that would be a surefire success is DogLand, an idea that I should take out some kind of patent on, but because dogs are naturally generous, I freely give to anybody who wants to make it happen.

There are three parts of DogLand: WaterLand, Grass-Land, and MudLand. There will be rides of course, but mainly to keep the humans busy, because they bore easily. WaterLand and GrassLand are fun, but personally, I'm going directly to MudLand. Not too many humans will be visiting MudLand; not because they don't want to, but because they have trouble doing anything natural. They will worry about getting their clothes dirty.

Well, that's fine. They would only get in the way. And certainly their clothes *would* get dirty, even if they couldn't bring them-

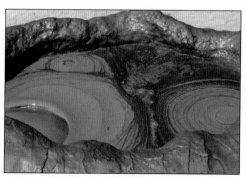

selves to jump in and roll around because dogs are jumping in and rolling around, then getting up and shaking themselves

MudLand

off, before jumping in for some more rolling around. I'm getting a little excited here just *thinking* about MudLand!

Admission to DogLand would be free on Opening Day, as a promotional thing. But after that, there would be a hefty entrance fee. Except on Dog Day. On Dog Day, it's free. You could get a Three-Day Pass because there just aren't enough hours in one day to do everything you'd want to do. So there's a Dog Hotel connected to DogLand, and a monorail, which goes directly from the hotel right into the park. And the entire family goes on a Family Pass; hell, even the cat can go, but cats never want to go anyplace, never mind a fun place like DogLand. But *if* one wanted to go, DogLand would be open to it. That's just the kind of place it is: generous and welcoming.

The Dog Channel: A Some-what Oustandingly Excellent Idea

We have much better things to do with our time than sit around watching TV. That said, we live in the real world. In the real world, your home has at least one, probably several TV sets, and your humans watch it for many hours every day, even though they're constantly complaining that "there's nothing good on." True enough, but there *could* be something good on. Specifically: the Dog Channel.

Let's start with what will *not* be on the Dog Channel. There will be *no* shows featuring phony "Dog Whisperers" or other charlatans offering advice on how to subjugate, humiliate, and manipulate dogs, euphemistically called "training" your dog. Instead, there will be interesting, informative dog news and documentaries, amusing dog comedies, gripping dog dramas, and a few trashy dog reality shows because everybody loves reality shows.

There will be shows like *Real Housedogs*, following six dogs living in a house on the New Jersey shore: their ups and downs, the inevitable personality conflicts, the eating, the sleeping, the barking, and did I mention the eating?

There will be reruns of the dated but still popular sitcom, *Love That Dog!* all about a frisky Golden Retriever puppy and all the trouble he gets himself into every week. Also the sophisticated, *Dog Friends*, about six dogs living in a Manhattan apartment, who obsess over the mundane details of their lives, rehashing every bone they've eaten and nap they've taken.

Animal Hospital would be a one-hour medical drama about the life-and-death struggles of sick and injured dogs; *NYPDK-9* the heart-in-your-throat cop thriller about police dogs confronting dangerous criminals, and also their own, messy personal lives. Sports fans will want to follow the Greyhound Races and also Dog Water Polo, where a bunch of dogs will go after a big ball in a swimming pool. (The Dog Water Polo Association is already working on the rules, but I've heard there won't be any.)

Here's the primetime lineup:

	8:00	**9:00**	**10:00**
Monday	*Dog Friends*	*Real Housedogs*	*Lost Dogs*
Tuesday	*Love That Dog!*	*NYPDK-9*	*Animal Hospital*
Wednesday	*Dog Water Polo*	*Rescue Dogs*	*60 Minutes till Dinner*
Thursday	*Real Housedogs*	*Everybody Loves Buster (Thursday edition)*	*The Bone Hour*
Friday	*Sleeping News*	*The Pound*	*Chew That Shoe!*
Saturday	*Dog Park*	*Barking Today*	*Two and a Half Dogs*
Sunday	*The Dobermans*	*Mad Dogs*	*Dancing with the Dachshunds*

This would be a pretty powerful lineup in my opinion, probably beating the other networks most nights. Sponsors would be falling all over themselves to buy commercial time.

I'm envisioning mostly dog food makers, but also dog restaurants and dog resorts, which by the time the Dog Channel gets off the ground, would be well-established. Really, it's a business plan that almost writes itself.

Questions That Could Theoretically Be Asked, Even Though They Aren't

Q: Can dogs fly?

A: Contrary to what you might think, dogs do not actually fly, but we do have an on-again-off-again relationship with gravity.

This dog is not flying.

Neither is this one.

Q: It looks like they're flying. Especially the one on the left.

A: Yes, but aerodynamically, it's just not possible. In theory, there's enough wingspan on the ears of a basset hound, but they just don't run fast enough to create enough lift for take-off.

Q: But I've seen it! Look, here's proof!

A: Well, I'm sorry, but that is just a digitally enhanced image. Really, they do not fly.

Reminders

Don't put all your bones in one hole. The reason for this is simple: You might forget where you put them. That would mean you would have to dig up the whole back yard and the whole front yard, looking for your one bone hole. But if you put every bone in a hole of its own, even if you forget where, you can start digging randomly and you'll probably find a bone; maybe not the one you were looking for, but some bone.

There's an interesting human variant on this idea, but like most human things, it doesn't make much sense: Don't put all your eggs in one basket. Today, humans mostly don't carry eggs in baskets, they carry them in these funny-shaped cardboard containers, but even if they did carry them in baskets, it wouldn't make much sense to carry them in two baskets instead of one. Because if they fell down, the eggs in both baskets would still break, right?

Really the whole egg thing is strange. The only good part is when they do drop them, which happens a lot, you get to eat them. They won't get down on the floor with you, because once they've dropped one on the floor and it's broken, they totally lose interest in that particular egg. This is one of the many reasons why you should always watch your humans closely, especially around the kitchen or dining areas, because they do drop food on the floor, and if you're reasonably quick, it can be in your stomach before they even *think* about picking it up; before the sound waves of the food hitting the floor even reach their inferior ears.

Q: Why are their ears inferior to ours?

A: Technically, this isn't a Q&A, this is a Reminder, but I'll take the question. Their ears are small, and they have no muscles to lift them up, or point them in any direction, as we do. Also, they can only hear sounds in a very limited frequency, and relatively close by. Often, we can sense danger approaching at a considerable distance so we rise up, turning our ears in the appropriate direction, and begin to bark. The humans have no idea that their home may be in danger! Fortunately, there will be other dogs in the neighborhood who will also bark to alert everybody about the problem.

Take Your Dog to Work Day

I'm not saying you should take your dog to work because we're bored at home. I'm telling you that a recent study shows that bringing dogs to work reduces stress. So really, it shouldn't be one special day that should be set aside for this. *Every* day should be Bring Your Dog to Work Day.

According to Professor Rudolph Barker, a professor of Management at Virginia Commonwealth University Business

School, "Pet presence can be a low-cost wellness-intervention." Clearly, there should be a statue of this man erected in the quad. There should also be one in front of The Virginia Commonwealth University School of Medicine and a third in the lobby of the Athletic Department, in case the first two aren't seen by enough students at the other locations.

Special attention should be paid to the phrase "low-cost" because in these difficult times, everybody needs to cut costs. Also, pay attention to the phrase "wellness-intervention" because every sick day results in lost productivity and

Quad at Virginia Commonwealth University Business School, which would be enhanced by a statue of Professor Barker. Okay, okay. It's not actually Virginia Commonwealth, it's the quad at Magdalene College, Oxford University. But Professor Barker's statue would also enhance this quad.

decreased profits, which in turn affect tax revenues, adding to the deficit. All of these bad things can be prevented simply by bringing your dog to work.

Instead of writing indecipherable prescriptions for dangerous drugs whose side effects are unknown despite premature approval by the FDA, doctors ought to have a clearly legible stamp that says, "BRING YOUR DOG TO WORK." That would be an actual wellness-intervention.

Here is a statue of Professor Barker and his dog, Sparky, which should be in the quad at either Virginia Commonwealth or Oxford University, or both. Technically speaking, it's not Professor Barker and his dog, Sparky. Technically, it's Franklin D. Roosevelt and his dog, Fala. But excessive worry about which man and which dog are portrayed in these statues causes exactly the kind of stress that is relieved by bringing your dog to work.

The Dog Party

First, you have to make a list of your invitees, then you have to set a date, then send out the invitations, then get the booze, then . . . Wait! I'm describing a *human* party, not a dog party! Dogs don't *plan* parties. Guess why?

Because whenever there are three or more dogs in the same place, *that's* a dog party! It could be indoors, it could be outdoors, on the street, in a park, on the banks of a river, anywhere at all where dogs meet, anytime, anyhow: PARTY!

Dog party

Somewhat larger dog party

There's no agonizing over who should or should not be invited. All dogs are equally welcome. I'm always happy to see another dog, even a tiny little Pomeranian or one of those toy dogs who really are dogs, down deep inside their miniature little souls.

So Pomeranians are welcome, St. Bernards are welcome, and all breeds and mixes in between. Happy to see you, friend! Let's get to sniffing each other's butts!

Is booze a necessary ingredient to ease the social flow? It is not. However, if some dog or human wants to bring some food, that would be an excellent idea, and it would make the party even more enjoyable. One outstanding type of get-together is the Bring Your Own Bone party.

How about this coming Saturday? Even better, how about: *Right now! Right here!*

Xtreme Sports for Dogs

This title is a little misleading since dogs do not require Xtreme sports. Before we explain this concept more completely, it's necessary to pose the following quiz:

What animal invented suicide?

A) Rabbits

B) Turtles

C) Elephants

D) Chickens

E) Humans

If you guessed "humans," you're right! And ever since they first came up with this spectacularly human idea, they've been trying to think of reasons not to commit suicide, since they hate their miserable lives and are always daydreaming about ending them. It would never occur to a turtle to commit suicide, even though turtles do not, in my opinion, share the *joi de vivre* that we dogs experience every moment of our waking lives. I could be wrong about this. Maybe in their own reptilian way, they have *joi*. Sometimes, when they sway their tiny little heads around like they do, they might be experiencing something joy-like.

Anyway, here's why you have to understand the whole concept of suicide to understand Xtreme human sports, like jumping out of airplanes or off bridges, or climbing up sheer rock faces: Humans invented these opportunities for themselves to face death, so that however briefly, they are shocked into an appreciation of life. Bungee jumping, for example. In this activity, a human attaches a long rubber band to his feet, then jumps off a bridge. As he hurtles towards the river below at 32 feet per second, per second, he realizes that he could die, if everything doesn't go absolutely perfect, and suddenly he wants to live!

Rock climbing is a little like this, only slower. Your human rock climber finds a sheer rock face hundreds of feet high and starts climbing up until he's high enough that if he slips and falls, he's going to die. Now, suddenly, he feels alive! Every moment becomes an intense experience and every move must be carefully calculated so he doesn't fall off the cliff.

Less athletically fit humans jump out of airplanes. Like the bungee jumpers, they get to experience hurtling towards the Earth at 32 feet per second, per second, and then as they get increasingly close, they pull a rip cord on their parachute, and if all goes well, it opens, and maybe they only break an ankle. If it doesn't go so well, they die, which is arguably what they wanted in the first place.

Another way for humans to have a good time is to jump out of a helicopter on a pair of skis, usually causing an avalanche. This looks like more fun than rock climbing to me, but in order for a dog to have a pretty fabulous time in the snow, no helicopters or avalanches are required. Just let us loose in some snow and you will understand the concept of fun. No equipment of any kind required, no skis, no snow boards, no chair lifts, and certainly not any helicopters. Just a dog and some snow.

Dogs do not require near-death experiences in order to love life. We love life simply by waking up in the morning and smelling it.

Do Dogs Have Consciousness?

The question here should be, but never is, do humans have consciousness? Of course dogs have it. But humans think

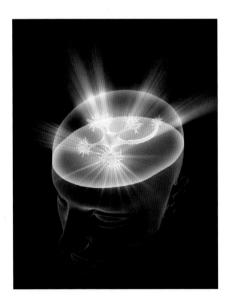

This image is typical of what you get when you look for illustrations of consciousness. Trust me, you will find no dogs with luminous rays emanating from their heads and reaching out into the universe. You will also find assorted silly photographs of people assuming yoga positions, my favorite of which is on a golf course. There is no location in this or any other dimension that is less spiritual than a golf course. A strip club is more spiritual.

that having it is what separates them from the lower animals. Ha, ha, ha.

Although I'm willing to entertain dissenting opinions from other dogs, my hunch is that humans definitely do *not* possess consciousness. They do possess self-consciousness, in that they are very self-conscious, that is to say embarrassed, by natural things like sex. But an understanding of where they fit into the world? No. They don't have a clue.

The Strategic Bone Reserve: When?

Humans are very prudent about preparing for future disasters, like maybe there won't be enough gas for them to drive their cars around in pointless circles, so they get ready for this by hiding large quantities of oil somewhere secret in the Strategic Oil Reserve. I have no objection to this, but what about a real catastrophe, like a sudden and unexpected interruption in the world supply of bones? What provision has been made for that? There is none! Clearly, this is a potential disaster which cries out for action.

A hospital that experiences a power outage? They have emergency backup generators. A famine or drought in Africa?

There are emergency food supplies and international aid agencies ready to respond. But what are we going to do if the world supply of bones crashes?

We need to have a Strategic Bone Reserve. Of course, the location of the Strategic Bone Reserve needs to be just as secret as the location of the Strategic Oil Reserve. In fact, it needs to be more secret. Can you imagine the chaos if its location were to leak out? Dogs from everywhere would descend upon it simultaneously and a World Dog Panic would occur, with attendant catastrophes in the human world. Banks would collapse, governments would fall; so the location must be a secret of the highest classification.

A World Dog Commission should appoint a Strategic Bone Reserve Location Committee, which would be charged with finding a secret location for the reserve. It would be made up of senior dogs from every nation in the world, whose

Dog sleeping uneasily, knowing the Strategic Bone Reserve does not yet exist.

integrity could not be questioned. Then, the reserve would be filled up with bones, which could be released in a crisis, but only by the World Dog Commission.

Until these actions are taken, dogs all over the world should not sleep well at night.

Dog sleeping easily, knowing the Strategic Bone Reserve is under construction.

To a human who can't tell the difference between a dog whose sleep is clearly troubled, and a dog who is sleeping in an untroubled way, these photographs may not be easily differentiated, but any dog could tell you what's going on here.

Moving

Humans consider moving one of life's most stressful experiences. It certainly is for dogs. One day everything is going along in a familiar pattern, and the next day everything is being packed up in boxes, and the furniture is being moved. What are you going to do with the bones you've buried? Where *are* the bones you've buried? You're going to have to start digging randomly—the flower garden is probably a good place to start, but even if you find a lot of them, there's no guarantee your humans will pack them up nicely for you in one of their boxes.

Sometimes humans will use the moving event as an excuse to get rid of some furniture, and you can be pretty sure it will be the best stuff, like your Comfortable Couch. A new place can mean new furniture. There's nothing worse than a new couch. It comes wrapped in plastic and is covered with noxious chemicals. It can take weeks to get rid of that chemical new couch smell. You're going to have to roll around in the mud, then quickly come back inside and roll around on the couch. Your humans won't like it, but you have to do this.

Then there's the whole problem of the new neighborhood and making new friends. There might be a Crazy Dog Neighbor up the street. There might be fewer good peeing trees, fire hydrants, or bushes. But I don't want to be too negative. You might be moving to a better neighborhood with better peeing trees, who knows?

All I can say is that I'm getting stressed out just thinking about moving, so we should move on to the next subject right away.

Politics

There is only one political issue worth debating, and that is: What should be done about cats? Unfortunately, there is no clear solution. Some dogs think that cats should be exterminated, and while the imagination soars at the prospect of a world without cats, the problem is how to get from here to there? I am normally against violence, except in self defense, and firmly opposed to murder.

One workable approach comes from an unlikely source: veterinarians. They propose neutering all cats, as a condition of adopting them. This idea has merit, the only problem being that they have the same idea about dogs. They seem unable to see the difference between dangerous cat overpopulation and maintaining a healthy population of dogs. Going down this road will lead to trouble.

There is a similar problem with the predator solution. Yes, mountain lions and coyotes could naturally reduce the cat population, but they are also dangerous to dogs. Mountain lions, for example, are essentially big cats, and can't be trusted. Coyotes are more like dogs, but there's really no feeling among them of solidarity with dogs. Actually, when you look into the eyes of a coyote, you sometimes see that same, predatory coldness you can see in a cat's. A hungry coyote looks at a small dog in the same way he looks at any smaller animal. I have said a few critical things about miniature dog breeds (which were uncalled for, I know), but whatever you may think of them, they are, technically speaking, dogs. I cannot approve of coyotes eating them.

This leaves us only with the power of prayer. I wish I could believe that the Great Dog answers prayers in a specific way, but I think He moves in more mysterious ways. Not that you shouldn't pray to him to take care of the cat problem, just don't hold your breath about it.

Social Networking for Dogs: Sniffing and Peeing in the Twenty-First Century

Dog Tweets

That hamburger I found? Way old! Puking it up now. #myhorribleday

Wow, somebody peed over my marker! ☹ #problems?

Digging up flowers in the neighbor's yard. What cd go wrong? #daydreaming

Smells like that cute Golden couple blks over is in heat. C U L8TR #datenite

Those Pomeranians barking at me from behind that big fence? They'd better hope their humans don't ever leave their gate unlatched. #petpeeves

Facebook for Dogs

I have this dilemma: I get messages from other dogs I don't know who want to friend me. I look at their pictures and don't recognize them. I don't want to be rude or insult them, but who *are* these dogs? There is one way I could verify their identity: if I could smell their butts. Then I'd know who they are. But for all their fancy technology, humans currently have no way to transfer scents over phone lines or satellites. When is this needed advance going to happen? Where's the research funding? They spend billions developing bioweapons and other stupid, dangerous stuff, and nothing on long distance odor transfer; it's like we're still stuck in the eighteenth century.

Probably it's because there is no obvious link to Defense Spending, where all the money is. Fine: we'll invent something: odor-transfer technology that can help a highly-trained military dog, sniff out whether a terrorist suspect in Afghanistan is or is not a terrorist, from a secure location on a military base in Kansas. When the Pentagon sees just how valuable this technology can be, they will fund it, and then I can use it to figure out who I really know and who I don't know on Facedog.

Well, that wasn't much of a chapter, so let's see what we have in the way of excuses for non-existent or barely-existent chapters. How about:

Another Lame Excuse

We have already discussed how writing certain chapters is like seeing some roadkill from a distance, getting kind of excited because it looks edible, or at least chewable, then getting right up to it and seeing that it's just so old and smashed into the road that you can't even get anything from licking it.

For humans who may be reading this book and did not respond to the whole roadkill thing with, "Oh! I've been there!!" I have a more relatable analogy: Let's suppose that you were at a party last night, and since you are so uncomfortable in any situation requiring you to interact socially with another human, you got very drunk. This had the intended consequence that you felt more relaxed, but the unintended consequence that you woke up this morning and there was somebody in bed with you, who you don't remember very well from the night before, but you thought this person was a lot more attractive and interesting than he or she turned out to be in the harsh light of morning.

So think of this chapter like that. When we first met the concept in the Table of Contents, it looked very attractive, but that's because everybody was drunk. Now, it's morning and everybody is stone cold sober. This chapter is going to have to get its clothes on as quickly as possible and get the hell out of here. Not to be unpleasant or anything, but just, you know, ASAP.

Common Myths about Dogs

Dog Obesity. There is no such thing as a fat dog. This myth, like many others, was made up and is spread by those purveyors of myths and misinformation: veterinarians.

There are only two kinds of dogs: your well-fed dog and your under-fed dog. I cannot recall ever meeting a dog I'd describe as fat. Robust maybe, large-boned, even stout, but never fat. You can't overfeed a dog. This canard has its origins in humans overfeeding themselves and each other. This I have seen. In fact, I've been a very reluctant witness to humans eating way too much food, stuffing themselves really, while I waited patiently for the gorging to end so I could clean up all the food they shouldn't be eating.

This dog is not fat. It is a well-fed dog.

Even humans describe this behavior as gluttony, one of the Seven Deadly Sins. Even among secular humans, they have no sooner overfed themselves than they are consumed with regret. Because they know they're all way too fat.

Dogs are lazy. Again, I have to say I've never met a lazy dog. I've occasionally met a dog whom I'd describe as "well-rested." But dogs have no concept of lazy, another idea from the humans' own list of deadly sins, this one called "sloth." It's a word that has gone out of common usage, when in fact it should be revived and used all the time to describe humans, but not dogs.

If a human encounters a dog who seems a bit listless—not moving around much and not interested in going out to the park for a romp and frisk—that human should examine the dog more closely to determine whether or not that dog is still alive. Nine out of ten times, you're looking at a deceased dog. If it's not moving, it's probably dead. So before casting aspersions on Spot, hold a mirror up to his nose and see if there's any breath coming out of him.

"That dog needs a bath." How many times have you heard that one? The whole concept of "bathing" is a social construct ripped from the dysfunctional world of the human and misplaced into the functional dog world. When a human stops smelling like a bar of perfumed soap (for like maybe a second or two) she typically takes a shower. While in the shower, she removes the natural coating of oils that has given her hair a healthful sheen, and washes it with at least two different "hair care products" including, but not limited to, shampoos and conditioners. Then, of course, when she's dried her hair with an energy-wasting blow dryer, it now lacks the natural sheen she washed away, so she has to use *other* hair care products to replace it.

This ritual is idiotic beyond belief, but you know what? If humans want to do this to themselves, let them. *Sobre gustos no hay nada escrito.* However, why subject dogs to this indignity? Without the natural protections afforded to us by the oils in our fur, we're subject to illness and death. All because of the crazy idea of giving your dog a bath.

And one more thing. Contrary to human belief, an unbathed dog is not only healthier, it is healthier *for human babies.* A study published recently in *Pediatrics,* which I read frequently, proves that children who live with dogs during the first year of life get sicker less frequently than kids from pet-free homes. There is a similar finding for children who live with cats, but it is *significantly weaker* than the result for dogs. Babies who lived with dogs were *31 percent* more likely to be in good health and babies who lived with cats only *6 percent* (basically within the margin of error).

Also noteworthy: Dogs who go outside the most and bring the most dirt back into the home are the healthiest dogs for kids to be around. Scientists believe that these dogs help babies develop their immune systems faster. So really, the idea "Let's give the dog a bath" should be amended to "Let's give the dog a bath and jeopardize the health of our baby! Let's compromise our baby's immune system!"

There Is No Such Thing as a Stupid Question. Ask!

Q: Sometimes you see humans walking on their own, without a dog. Why?

A: It is not known why they do that. Of course, they are disadvantaged in an important way since they don't have a dog, but beyond that there is no logical reason why they are found walking on sidewalks.

Q: Are there any theories?

A: They are not marking their territory, this much we know. They have been observed peeing on trees or walls, but only because they're drunk and have weak bladders. There's no *purpose* to it.

Q: Maybe they're looking to meet other humans?

A: Not on the street, without a dog. One of the main reasons why single humans get dogs is because dogs help them meet other single humans walking their dogs.

Q: How?

A: The dogs being walked by the humans are naturally friendly and curious, so they will immediately start smelling each other's butts. This becomes a reason, which they don't normally have, to start talking to each other.

Q: About the butt smelling?

A: No, they won't do that. One of them will open up a conversation saying something like, "Is that a German Shepherd?" when it's perfectly obvious to anyone that it is.

Q: Then what happens?

A: The other human will say, "Yes. I got him when he was eight weeks old, he's a really sweet dog, and so devoted to me! What kind of dog is yours?"

Q: And then the humans mate?

A: No, they have to arrange to meet later on, normally at least a day or two later, and then they go somewhere where they can get drunk enough to talk with each other. *Then* they mate.

Q: But why do they walk without dogs?

A: The only explanation I've heard has to do with "exercise," a strange behavior they engage in because most of the time they just sit around doing really pointless things, so they need to exercise or else they will get really fat, instead of just kind of fat, which they already are.

Q: Maybe they want to smell the world?

A: They have almost no sense of smell, and they never sniff anything while walking. Once in a blue moon a human will sniff a rose, if it's right in front of her, but bending down or sniffing around a tree to see who has peed there? No way.

Q: What about "jogging"?

A: There is no known explanation for "jogging." Dog experts have studied humans engaged in this activity but

Do these humans look happy?

have not come up with an explanation. Videos of humans have always shown the same result: Humans who are jogging are always miserable. There is nothing about this which makes them happy, and everything about it which makes them unhappy.

Q: Then why do they do it?

A: Why do they do anything they do?

Exceptions to Rules

There's nothing as boring as a bunch of rules. The only thing rules are good for is breaking. However, in terms of lists (also inherently boring), there's an exception, and that exception is a list of exceptions to rules, so here's my list:

1. Always fight boredom, except when watching a Dog Show. In that case you should completely surrender to boredom, let boredom wash over you like a giant wave. If you don't, you will be consumed with righteous anger and we don't want to encourage any negativity in this book.

2. Always pay attention in class, except when the teacher or the subject is boring, and you will notice that if one of them is, the other usually is also. A class you may be subjected to is Dog Obedience Class. Just let your mind wander, think about events that have happened or might happen, places you've peed or will pee, what

the Obedience Trainer would look like wearing a choke collar you could yank, etc.

3. Never bite the hand that feeds you, except if that same hand is yanking on a choke collar in a sadistic attempt to control your behavior and subjugate your spirit. That hand you may and should bite.

4. Never write a run-on sentence, except when you happen to feel like writing one, in spite of a bunch of stupid rules of writing that were written decades ago by humans who are now long dead, in books like *The Elements of Style*, which I'm sure you'll agree is an insufferably snotty title for a book, not that I have anything against E.B. White, who wrote *Charlotte's Web*, among many other fine books, but who the hell is William Strunk Jr., I'd like to know, because anybody with a name like William Strunk Jr. is not to be trusted on any subject, much less the delicate and personal subject of writing about dogs.

5. All lists should have at least ten items, except when you can't think of ten, like now. If I added five more just to pad the list so it would come out to ten exceptions instead of five, I would be straining to come up with stuff and giving bad advice to impressionable young dogs, a betrayal of my readers for which I would be guilty of literary negligence, a criminal offense.

More Dog Haiku

Chewing on a bone.
You've got troubles? I don't care.
I'm a happy dog.

Frolic though you may,
A dark spirit doth loom near.
I smell cat litter.

You didn't throw it.
Is fooling me that funny?
You, sir, are a prick.

Heavy is the mind,
Eminent mortality.
Niche might . . . DOORBELL!!!

Mud is on the couch.
Your face and hands are now licked.
You're welcome my friend.

Another Pop Quiz

What animal invented bottled water, which is basically tap water (the kind which has already been filtered to remove the noxious chemicals which that same animal dumped into the rivers and lakes from which the water was taken, so it's now perfectly healthy and safe to drink) then put it into fancy plastic bottles with colorful labels calling the tap water "Mountain Spring-Fed Babbling Brook" and then charged actual money for it, which others are delighted to pay?

Was your answer goats? I'm sorry, but goats did not invent bottled water. Guess again.

Did you guess giraffes? No, giraffes didn't invent bottled water either.

How about beavers? After all, beavers are water experts since they live in water and build clever dams in it. Unfortunately, while beavers are a good guess, beavers did not invent bottled water.

Here's which animal invented it: the human, that's who. And whoever invented and marketed this stuff is now a very, very rich person because it's been a smashing success. To paraphrase one of the great human philosophers, nobody has ever lost money underestimating the intelligence of the human being.

Better Land Use for Both Dogs and Humans

Let's start with gyms. There's a lot of wasted land taken up by places with weird machines humans use in a hopeless attempt to make themselves more fit. The reason that they're not fit is because a) they eat way too much, and b) they don't get any normal exercise. Gyms sometimes have swimming pools, which is okay, but everything else should go and be replaced by dirt or grass. They could romp on the dirt and grass, and there'd be a mud pit where they could roll around. If they needed to go to a mud-unfriendly place after that, they could shower off, which they do anyway as soon as they've "worked up a sweat" on one of their dumb machines.

One of the reasons they think they need gyms is because they spend what leisure time they have in unhealthful places like auditoriums, where hundreds or even thousands of them sit and watch one or two of them standing up on the stage and making noise, or even just talking, and they can't even do that without amplification. At least the performers should shout, that would be a little exercise. I'd replace these with poopatoriums, where dogs would come to poop. This could solve the Poop Problem, and of course I'm not talking about dogs having problems pooping, which we do not, I'm talking about humans scooping it up into plastic bags before we've had a chance to smell it, never mind any *other* dog's poop. So our humans would take us to these poopatoriums, where it'd be okay to poop and smell each other's.

A similar venue is a stadium—normally used for sporting events—where a small number of humans who are designated as the athletically fit ones, engage in team competitions while the vast majority sit down to watch them, often drinking beer, because it's too boring to watch unless they're also drunk. If they can't justify building these things unless organized sports happen in them, my idea for a dog sport is that dogs would be divided into two teams, one on each side of a white line. Somebody would blow a whistle and everybody would start to poop, then somebody would blow another whistle and we'd stop. The referees would then count the poops, and whichever team had the most would win. Then we'd all get to run around and roll in the mud, and the humans could clean up the poop if they wanted to.

And finally, there is the shopping mall, where at least there is some walking. But of course there are levels, and to get up to say the fourth level, humans might actually climb some stairs, which would be healthy, except that, surprise! A human invented the escalator a long time ago so they don't have to do that anymore. They just get on this thing and suddenly they're on the fourth floor, where the Mrs. Fatty's Cookie Shoppe is.

Once they've consumed way too many cookies, they get back on the escalator. They don't even exercise the muscles they might have used going *down* the stairs! Sometimes you have to wonder why the Great Dog created humans. He could have given the job of providing food and shelter for dogs to the horses. He'd have had to make horses smarter than they are, in fact a whole *lot* smarter, but at least a horse would not have invented the escalator, nor would a horse ride on one. I know I have never seen a horse on an escalator.

The Education of a Dog

A dog's education is not an endless, arduous ordeal characterized by boredom, humiliation, and resentment. That is the human model. For a dog, education comes quickly and easily by curiosity, observation, and experience. It is a joyous thing, informed by smelling the goodness of the world. A puppy carefully observes her elders and quickly learns what to do and how to do it. In a matter of months, she will be ready to be out on her own, and after a year or two, when a human is still pooping in his pants and yowling constantly, a dog is a young adult.

Nevertheless, capable as she is, she is still learning, still curious; the adventure of lifelong learning never ends for a dog

By contrast, let's return to the human model. First there is the enslavement of what is euphemistically called K–12, which means no less than thirteen years of servitude, usually preceded by a couple of years of "pre-school" readiness training, a gentle period of gradually lowering expectations. Then the serious boredom and humiliation begins.

(A note: there are a few multiple-choice tests scattered throughout this book, but while I believe some of the choices may be better than others, you will not be graded, and I freely admit other choices than the one I would pick may also be good choices. These are merely review opportunities.)

Those humans who survive K–12, and whose families can afford it, will then go off to college, where they can pursue serious studies in drinking. Relatively speaking, college is the best of the human educational experiences, and some of the students remain sober enough to graduate after four or five years, an occasion where everybody wears remarkably silly hats.

Below are a few hats. Guess which one is the hat worn by the most educated humans at their graduation.

Does this make you think "Gaudeamus igitur"?

How about this one?

To me, this one says, "I know something you
don't. Or else, why would I be wearing this hat?"

Actually, it's this one.

The odd thing is, that if the human then chooses to continue on to "graduate school," it actually turns out to be a return to the boredom, humiliation, and resentment of high school. The only possible reason to go to grad school is so they can wear brightly-colored red and purple sashes on top of the medieval black robes at graduation ceremonies. Of course, by the time humans get through all of this, they are no longer young, and unlike dogs, their brains are no longer spongy and absorbent enough to learn anything. Occasionally, when they're elderly, they try pathetically to recapture their youth by taking Emeritus classes. Emeritus is a Latin word meaning "really old."

Fortunately, dogs don't have to take classes for lifelong learning. For us, life *itself* is a class in lifelong learning. This book is not really *needed* by dogs, who educate themselves. It's like a delicious bone with a lot of meat still on it, discovered at the bottom of a garbage can, overturned by a vigilant dog.

Even More Dog Haiku

Hell hath no fury
Like the scorn of a feline.
You do not fool me.

"Roll over," you barked
And I cheerfully obliged.
Prime rib would be nice.

Tiger burning bright.
What immortal hand or eye
Screwed up so badly?

A stranger passes,
Human companion ignores.
Hey, that guy had food.

No screeching, no claws,
All's quiet and peaceful now.
A world without cats.

The Dilemma of "No"

I realize that elsewhere in this book I said that the human word "No!" when directed towards a dog has no functional or operational meaning. This is not always true.

How can something be true and also not true? The answer to this puzzle can be found in the wisdom of our mysterious eastern dog cousins in India and China. According to their beliefs, it's possible. I admit I don't fully understand the concept, but as it applies to "No!" on rare occasions, you should listen and obey this command.

For example, suppose you're outside in your front yard. You're thirsty and you notice a small, shallow pool of liquid. It's not water, but it's certainly wet, and so you're going to have some, and suddenly you hear the dreaded "No!" command. Naturally, you're inclined to ignore it, but on this occasion you should obey, because your human knows something you don't: this liquid is a noxious chemical poison which your human has been using in a misguided attempt to turn the meadow area out front into a barren monoculture known as a "lawn." This can't be done without chemical poisons, and if you drink any of it, you're going to see the last person on Earth you want to see: the vet. And the vet will do unmentionable things to you in a typical overreaction to the problem.

If you're not sure if the "No!" you've just heard is one you can ignore or not, clues are available. You should listen to the sound quality of the human's voice. If it's merely angry, chances are you can ignore, but if it's flavored with hints of hysteria or panic, you should probably obey. Humans are always talking about their wines and beers being flavored with "hints" of pear, apple, honeysuckle, green pepper, and other nonsense. Their beers and wines are flavored with one thing: alcohol, and it ain't subtle, which is why they like it, not because of the hint of honeysuckle. But the flavorings behind their "No!" *can* be subtle, so you should listen closely.

If you hear no hint of panic, you can treat the "No!" like the distant call of a seagull, floating on extended wings above a far-away beach. *Ca-a-a-w! Ca-a-a-w! Ca-a-a-w!* Poignant, lovely, but having nothing to do with you.

More Common Myths about Dogs

A very common one is the Myth of the Bad Dog. You hear humans scolding, "Bad dog!" all the time, usually because a dog is doing some perfectly natural thing. But there *is* no such thing as a bad dog. Misunderstood, maybe. Mistreated, occasionally. High-strung, sometimes, but never bad. Deep inside a misbehaving dog is a good dog, yearning to get out. Looking for that chance.

Maybe your "bad" dog is simply trying to send you an important message. Like: You're not spending enough quality time with your dog. This is why he has ripped all the stuffing out of your favorite couch. He is only asking for your attention. He is acting out. Or there could be a different issue. Perhaps your house is unsafe. You need to rewire the house before it burns down, maybe killing you and your family in the process. Your "bad dog" is scratching the walls to send you the message. Or maybe there is a personal issue in your family. Perhaps your son or daughter is addicted to drugs, and *you don't know about it!* This could be why he's chewed up your furniture. Probably that's it. You need to sit down with your teenager and start asking a few questions. The last thing you need to do is become distracted over the "bad dog" non-issue.

Another myth is the Myth of Spoiled Food. Any food in a human refrigerator is basically good to go, and by "go" I mean "eat." It may be *j-u-u-u-st* a little past its prime, the so-called "expiration date" stamped on the package may have come and gone, but that in *no way* means that it's "spoiled." Humans have developed an elaborate system of food "inspections" and labeling requirements overseen by a giant bureaucracy called the FDA, which is short for the Department of Totally Needless Paranoia. Somebody in Washington, D.C. decides if you can eat some perfectly good hamburger meat? What's that about? The idea that good food, a little old maybe, should be thrown away is an abomination. Look, Grandpa is a little past his prime, too. Would you throw Grandpa away?

Finally there is the Myth of the Good Dog. Why is this a myth? It's a myth because it suggests that *all* dogs are not good, only *some* dogs. Or that a dog is not good *all* of the time, only *some* of the time, and guess when *that* time is? Give up? It's when the dog is doing something the human wants it to do, or not doing something the human doesn't want it to do. These "good" dog behaviors are usually unnatural for the dog, which is why the humans try to reinforce it with false praise. It's really nothing more than manipulation and trickery. Really, if you buy into this, the result is that your self-esteem is *lowered*, not raised. Who decides when you're being good, and when you're being bad? *You* decide!

Dog Retirement

Just kidding!

Retirement is a human concept, a corollary to the equally human concept of work. You cannot retire from being a dog. You are a dog from the moment you enter this world to the moment you are reunited with the Great Dog.

Humans start to surrender their natural love of life when they first pass through the cold, dark gates of education. At one time this was mercifully delayed until they were six or seven years old, but now it starts almost immediately in preschool. They're too young to have life completely stomped out of them, but not too young to begin the dreary preparation for it.

School continues for the next twenty years or so, until their youth has been wasted, and then they are ready for work. The prime of their life is then given over to this work, but they cling to the hope that at some time in the future they can quit, and this is called "retirement." They don't realize that they could quit anytime, so they trudge on through their best years, until at last they can retire, but by then of course, it's too late. They are left with declining health, cognition, and vitality, mercifully ended by death.

A few lucky ones escape the grim cycle because they are unemployable. These fortunate souls at least have a chance at happiness, but there's other obstacles they must overcome, and unless they are surrounded by dogs, there's not much hope for them. Onto the treadmill in the bloom of youth, off it when any remaining competence has been wrung from them by senility.

Retired cat

There is really only one animal for whom retirement is appropriate, and that is a cat. A retired cat isn't as good as a dead cat, or a sleeping cat, but it's certainly better than an awake cat. A retired cat would not bother to chase mice, interfere with dogs, or even sharpen its claws. It would just lie around, which is mostly what a cat does, but sometimes they wake and cause trouble. A retired cat would never do that.

I would provide an image of a retired human here, but that would be too depressing, and also a retired dog, but there is no such thing as a retired dog.

The Rights of Dogs: Still Waiting

We hear way too much about human rights and the Bill of Rights and never anything about the Rights of Dogs. Probably this is because dogs have no rights. But we *should* have rights!

Let's start with the freedom to bark, then move along to the right to a prompt and speedy trial before a jury of dogs, the right to confront our accusers in a court of law, the right not to be forced to testify against ourselves, the right to cross-examine witnesses, and challenge the evidence.

Here is a typical situation:

This dog is clearly innocent. Yes, there is pee on the floor, but who knows how it got there? Someone could have peed in a jar in some other location, then snuck into the house and poured the pee on the floor. But never mind. Let's stipulate to the fact that someone has peed. But who? I look at this dog and I see a wrongfully accused animal. It could have been another dog, but far more likely it was a cat. Or even a human. It could have been somebody in the accuser's family, even the accuser herself! Let the jury consider that the accuser is not even shown completely, only her legs and pointing finger! There is no eye-witness testimony, only the flimsiest circumstantial evidence.

There is no proof, only prejudice, unwarranted assumptions, a rush to judgment.

And now let's move along to another tragedy about to happen. A cat has clearly upset a potted houseplant. Who do you think is going to be blamed for it? The dog, of course. The crime has just occurred and we see who is responsible. But by the time the humans arrive on the scene, the cat will be long gone. The dog is going to take the fall.

If I was defending this dog, I would call the cat as a hostile witness and shred its credibility on the stand. My client would be declared not guilty by a jury of his peers. But this will not happen. Because dogs have no rights. Yet. But one day, we will have rights. No dogs will be wrongfully accused and punished. The arc of history bends towards justice! One day, not in my lifetime, my puppies, but maybe in yours.

Meditation for Dogs

As I understand it, the point of meditation as practiced by humans is to quiet the constant yammering of the human voice inside the head of your average human. This voice is pretty much constant, subdued slightly when the human sleeps, but loud and insistent during its waking hours. I can well understand the desire to make this voice shut up.

The problem is: How? This has stumped spiritual seekers for thousands of years. The most profound teachers have come up with yoga, where the human sits in various uncomfortable positions that are supposed to help somehow, and they concentrate on breathing, sometimes using a *mantra,* a random bunch of nonsense syllables which will hopefully replace the yammering. Observe this photograph:

This human is very clearly not happy, and the reason is she's sitting in a very uncomfortable position on a bunch of rocks. She's probably thinking: "Will you take the f***ing photograph already so I can get off these

Not-happy human meditating

rocks and go home?" I can't see how this is going to quiet her inner voice.

But dogs also need to meditate. We don't have the same problem as humans do, since our inner monologue is about more important matters like what and when are we going to eat next. And possibly when and where can we seize our next Sleep Opportunity. Still, it would be nice to have no inner voice bothering us, even about weighty issues.

A dog's approach to meditation, however, starts by not getting into an uncomfortable position, because it becomes very difficult to think about anything other than how uncomfortable you are. So we look for a position which frees our spirit from physical concerns. Here is a dog meditating:

This is an advanced position, and puppies should prob-

ably not attempt it at first. But note the serenity. This dog has certainly quieted, if not completely silenced, his inner voice. He is floating somewhere on the astral plane, his dog spirit separate from his dog body.

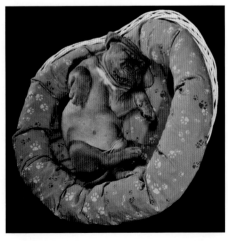

I think if human spiritual seekers would take dogs along with them to their yoga classes, they would benefit from the example we would set for them. It would be a lot more helpful than the yoga mat, which is one of the many odd things humans pay way too much money for, money which could be better spent buying excellent food for their dogs.

Instead, they go to these classes where everybody has brought yoga mats, and they secretly check out every other member of the class to see if he or she is fatter or thinner than they are, which gives them something to either worry or gloat about, which only distracts them more from the spiritual quest. Instead of that, they could be watching the Meditating Dog in the photograph above, and trying to position themselves more like the dog.

The Dog Entertainment Industry

Ha, ha! Fooled you! There is no such thing as the Dog Entertainment Industry because dogs don't need to be entertained. Even if you leave us alone in an entertainment-challenged environment, like your house, we'll find your shoes and chew on them for entertainment (see below).

Anyway, humans are not satisfied with themselves, their own lives, families, or friends, so they invent new friends they

pretend they have in books, plays, movies, and on TV. (We're not going to even try to explain the concept of alternate lives lived in games and other weird online communities.) If a dog is dissatisfied with his friends, he gets new ones. Humans, not so much. Hence, the Entertainment Industry.

For example, one of the most successful TV shows ever was called *Friends*. There were a bunch of young humans, all of whom were way more attractive than the humans watching them, and they pretty much just hung around an apartment. Of course, they weren't real humans, they were make-believe humans who were played by actors, who are also humans who don't have actual lives, but pretend to. If they're attractive enough, they become celebrities who then go on to have miserable lives followed closely by tabloid magazines, which provides some satisfaction to all the other the humans who are not celebrities.

But you should watch TV because at certain moments, the humans will get up from their couches and go into the kitchen. You also get up and follow them, because they're going there to get some more food they shouldn't be eating, and you can provide an alternate destination for that food. Or at least a supplementary destination, to help them feel a little less guilty. "Some for me, some for the dog."

Some Questions from the Back, Please

Okay, I'm seeing a lot of the same paws, and I'd like to see a few paws raised in the back row. Surely there are some puppies with questions back there. Yes?

Q: What is the most chewable thing?

A: Well, that's an excellent question! But there's no easy answer. It all depends on the dog. For example, a Pitt Bull will generally want something big and robust, assuming that there's no readily available bone to chew on. I'd recommend the kind of rope used to secure ships to a dock. But what about our smaller dog friends? The miniature dog breeds, (and yes, they *are* dogs, even though they don't necessarily *look* like dogs) will not be able to get their tiny jaws around a rope. So for them I'd recommend a leather shoe. Leather is something that was once part of a cow,

so while it's not meat or bone, it's got something of the cow left in it.

Q: What about a slipper?

A: Definitely chewable. Not in the same class as a leather boot, but you make do with what's available. Sometimes, humans will restrict access to leather shoes, especially after a few of them have been chewed up, so look around, and get creative.

Q: How long should you wait after peeing on something before peeing on something else?

A: There is no minimum amount of time. You may be called upon to mark something within less than a foot of something else you've marked, if another dog has marked it in your territory. So you have to have a reserve amount of pee at all times. This requires discipline and practice, but you have to resist the urge to pee out everything that's in your bladder on the first tree, wall, or fire hydrant you come across.

Q: How come there aren't more paintings and statues of dogs?

A: Most statues are of horses, but they don't count, because they're really statues of human generals and cavalry officers on horses. Then there are all those Egyptian statues of cats, but we believe they were made hoping the statues would scare mice away from their grain supplies, so they wouldn't actually have to get a real cat.

There are also paintings of hunting dogs, once very popular, but not much anymore, since hunting is no longer this big event with humans dressed in funny outfits riding horses and blowing horns. Now hunting is mostly humans dressed in funny outfits sitting in cold water waiting for ducks. Because this is intensely boring and cold, they generally start drinking, so you have to be very careful they don't shoot you, thinking you're a duck. They dress in bright red outfits so they won't shoot each other, but they still do, and when you consider how little another human with a gun, dressed in red, resembles a duck, you know you'd better be real careful not to make any sudden moves.

Q: How do you get to a cat that's in a tree?

A: To my knowledge there's no way to get to a cat in a tree. They have claws, we don't. On the other hand, while cats climb trees well, they're not so good at climbing down, so there's a lot of entertainment value in watching humans trying to get a cat down from a tree.

A Dog for Every Human

Every good human deserves a dog. Of course some humans can't devote the necessary time and attention to a dog, and for them a dog substitute like a statue can be used, but the only reason this is necessary is that dogs are still unwelcome in some extremely uptight workplaces. However, it is a proven fact (noted elsewhere in this book) that dogs in workplaces not only enhance the workplace in general, but also increase human productivity. So really, there is no reason why every good human should not have a dog.

Of course, there may be cats already living with a human, which can be a problem. So a reasonable question is: If I already have a cat, should I also get a dog? The answer is: Yes, unless your cat is especially vicious, in which case you should get rid of the cat, *then* get a dog. If your cat is just normally vicious, your new dog will have to figure out how to cope with it, and this can be done in most cases without killing the cat. Most, but not all cases.

Hopefully, you don't have a cat, so there really is no reason at all not to get a dog, a transformational event that will make your life so much more enjoyable, it's hard to imagine.

Which of the following humans do you think has a dog and which does not?

Well, that was kind of easy, because there's a dog in one of the pictures, but you can see what not having a dog is doing to the other human.

A recent study conducted at a prestigious university somewhere, not yet available to the general public, shows conclusively that the average life expectancy for a human who has a dog is dramatically higher (average: 104.2 years) than the life expectancy for a human without a dog (average: 58.7 years).

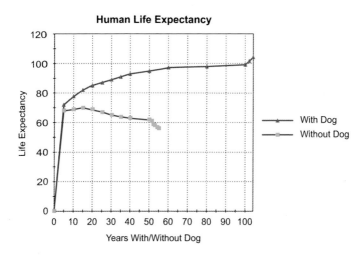

Human Life Expectancy

This graph speaks for itself. You can plainly see that human life expectancy goes way up, starting after spending just a few years with a dog, and continues to climb up to an average 104 years, while the more years spent without a dog, the fewer years a human can expect to live. So talk about preventive medicine! Instead of wasting all that money on pills, get a dog!

Correction

It has been brought to my attention that earlier in this book I wrote that the only cat you could trust is a dead cat. This may have overstated the case somewhat. More important, there may be cat lovers out there—and I know they do exist—who might be offended. If they *are* offended, they won't recommend this book to their friends, which would be bad. Everybody needs to recommend this book to their friends, and even to people they don't really like that much.

So I think what I meant to say was not that the only cat you can trust is a *dead* cat, but rather that the only cat you can trust is a *fed* cat. It was a typo! This makes a lot more sense. If a cat has not been fed, it's more likely to be cranky and make a sudden, unprovoked attack with its claws on an innocent and unsuspecting dog. But if a cat is *fed*, it's more likely to find a comfortable chair and go to sleep, which is much better for everybody. Now you have a cat which is asleep, not dead, but also not awake, so: better than awake, but not all the way too dead.

This cat is temporarily worthy of your trust, until it wakes up.

I hope I've cleared this up, and I do apologize to cat lovers for any misunderstanding that might have occurred due to this unfortunate typo.

The Dogma of Rufus: The TV Show

First, my puppies, now would be a good time to take a five-minute break. Go outside and romp. Play together, expressing the sheer joy of life and living, as you know how to do so well, without any instruction whatsoever.

And now for all you producers and network executives who are already thinking this book would make a great TV show: You are right. My advice: Act now with a preemptive offer which could take the rights to this off the table. If you wait for the book to be a big success, the price goes up, and suddenly you're in a bidding war. You don't want to be in a bidding war, so pick up the phone and call Skyhorse Publishing immediately. Go right to the top, demand to speak to Tony.

You don't have to make all the creative decisions now. Secure the rights, then you can decide whether to do it as an animation show, as live-action, or something in between. I will, of course, want script approval. If this is a problem for you, let me say that everything is on the table. Your people can talk to my people, and something can be worked out.

I am not an unreason-
able dog. That said, do not
think you can slip anything
by me regarding subsidiary
rights. The merchandising,
the t-shirts, the backpacks,
the action figures, the dolls,
the pajamas. We will be full
participants in all of that.

My agent

And just so you know,
on the subject of the defi-
nition of net profit: I wasn't
born yesterday.

Come the Revolution

I'm an old dog now, and my political views have moder-
ated. And yet, sometimes my heart quickens when I hear
the phrase, "Come the revolution . . ." Basically, my feeling
is that feeding and caring for humans would not be worth
the trouble. Things are better as they are. But still. On a lazy
afternoon as I drift off into my midday nap, I think about
those aisles in pet stores devoted to products to "control" your
dog, mostly costing anywhere from $100 to $300, which are
basically electronic collars that come with hand-held devices

to deliver electric shocks to your dog when it does something you don't like, or doesn't do something you *would* like. And this is what I dream about: rounding up all the humans who made, sold, bought, or used any of these devices, and fitting *them* with the collars.

Once the collars are in place, dogs would then control their humans and train them, for example, not to shout, or speak too loudly. It's not that we wouldn't allow them to talk quietly among themselves, just not shout or speak harshly in a way which could disturb the dog community. They would learn soon enough. And if they had any ideas about escaping, there would be an electrified fence surrounding the property.

Also, human restaurants would be replaced with dog restaurants, previously described in this book, and human resorts with dog resorts. We'd have dog newspapers and magazines, we'd celebrate Dog Day. There would be all kinds of improvements, come the revolution.

ABOUT THE AUTHOR

I don't like to bark much about myself, but here's a profile I put together for DogMatch.com:

I am a ruggedly handsome Bull Dog mix who enjoys chasing Frisbees and UPS guys, and long, romantic walks on the beach (no leashes). I'm seeking a female dog, any age, any breed, for a casual encounter.

Because I'm a dog and don't type well, I have asked some humans to assist me with this book.

These humans, Larry Arnstein and Zack Arnstein, have published three books, *The Dog Ate My Resumé*, *The Bad Driver's Handbook*, and *The Ultimate Counterterrorist Home Companion*. Their second book, which sold 15,000 copies, was made into a page-a-day desk calendar,

which sold about four times as many copies as the book. So they started writing calendars instead of books.

They've published seven of them, but one was just a calendar version of *The Bad Driver's Handbook*, so that one doesn't really count. They've asked another family member, Joey Arnstein, to help with the typing on this one.

CRITICAL PRAISE FOR *THE DOGMA OF RUFUS* FROM DOGS

"Probably the first, certainly the only book I know that presents dog issues in a serious and responsible manner."

—Buster, *Cleveland Dog Times*

"Nothing I've read previously compares. Rufus writes about mud with a unique and eloquent voice."

—Daisy, *Kansas City Dog Review*

"Riveting! . . . Couldn't put it down!"

—Rex, *Dog Magazine*

"Matches up favorably in my opinion with Dickens and Thackeray."

—Buddy, *Arf! Quarterly*

AFTERWORD: CRITICAL PRAISE FOR HUMAN TYPISTS' PREVIOUS BOOKS FROM HUMANS

I've looked over this book and I think the humans have done a pretty good job of typing, so I offer this in the way of a blurb: "Good humans!"

However, my typists have asked to have the following added as well:

The Detroit Free Press called *The Bad Driver's Handbook* "hysterically funny." *The Sunday Times of London* wrote, "It . . . reveals the rules of the road we all know to be true . . . [and] puts forth a compelling argument rarely acknowledged by traffic authorities." *Roadtrip America* called it "hilarious." *The Salt Lake Tribune* called it "The most indispensable book ever written for the motoring public." *BookPage* wrote, "Finally . . . takes a common, everyday bugaboo and turns it on its ear." Scotland's *Daily Record* said, "At last, the truth has been told." Canada's *National Post* called it "The funniest book ever penned on how to drive."

On NPR's *News and Notes with Ed Gordon,* Ferai Chideya called it, "Truly, really funny," and said the authors "Could end up with a Nobel Peace Prize."

Of *The Dog Ate My Resumé,* *USA Today* said, ". . . loaded with laugh-out-loud mock 'Do's' to ease your way into the working world . . . great pick-me-up reading." NPR commentator Sandra Tsing Loh wrote, "A hilarious and fast read." *Newsday's* Marvin Kitman wrote, ". . . such a useful and hilarious book, it made me want to go back to college."

Of *The Counterterrorist Home Companion*, Sean Gonsalvez, writing in the *Cape Cod Times* called it "a hilarious antidote to the fear-mongering fueling the 'war on terror.'" On his show, *Air America,* Thom Hartmann called it "A really funny read, it's a great book." Barry Lynn, on *Culture Shocks* said, "A very, very funny book . . . this is a great book."

PHOTO CREDITS

p. vi – WilleeCole/Shutterstock

p. ix, xii, 2, 12, 16, 28, 32, 38, 52, 58, 64, 92, 120, 152, 162, 166, 186, 192, 204 – iStockphoto/Thinkstock

p. xi – Shutterstock

p. 4 – John Howard/Lifesize/Thinkstock

p. 10 – iStockphoto/Thinkstock

p. 10 – Photodisc/Thinkstock

p. 14 – iStockphoto/Thinkstock

p. 15 – FogStock/Thinkstock

p. 17 – Vitaly Titov & Maria Sidelnikova/Shutterstock

p. 18 – Vitaly Titov & Maria Sidelnikova/Shutterstock

p. 19 – Anna Hoychuk/Shutterstock

p. 21 – Annette Shaff/Shutterstock

p. 22 – iStockphoto/Thinkstock

p. 23 – iStockphoto/Thinkstock

p. 24 –Marilyn M. Soper/Shutterstock

p. 24 – iStockphoto/Thinkstock

p. 25 – aquatic creature/Shutterstock

p. 30 – iStockphoto/Thinkstock

p. 31 – Thinkstock

p. 34 – iStockphoto/Thinkstock

p. 34 – iStockphoto/Thinkstock

p. 40 – Comstock/Thinkstock

p. 41 – Zoonar/Thinkstock

p. 41 – Digital Vision/Thinkstock

p. 42 – iStockphoto/Thinkstock

p. 45 – iStockphoto/Thinkstock

p. 46 – iStockphoto/Thinkstock

p. 47 – Comstock/Thinkstock

p. 48 – JPagetRFPhotos/Shutterstock

p. 51 – iStockphoto/Thinkstock

p. 55 – iStockphoto/Thinkstock

p. 56 – Monkey Business/Thinkstock

p. 60 – iStockphoto/Thinkstock

p. 60 – John Foxx/Stockbyte/Thinkstock

p. 66 – Ralf Juergen Kraft/Shutterstock

p. 66 – iStockphoto/Thinkstock

p. 67 – Nikolai Tsvetkov/Shutterstock

p. 68 – pixshots/Shutterstock

p. 69 – Utekhina Anna/Shutterstock

p. 71 – Liliya Kulianionak/Shutterstock

p. 73 – Eric Isselee/Shutterstock